Jónas Kristjánsson

Icelandic Sagas and Manuscripts

Jónas Kristjánsson

Icelandic Sagas
and Manuscripts

SAGA
PUBLISHING CO.
Reykjavik Iceland

ka þugla ok þaiʀ nam
gum se þ̈ komir. Oþui
ʀum mans þa ſk h mk

A New Land

The history of the Scandinavian North begins in the twilight of pre-history. Archæological evidence shows these lands to have been inhabited for thousands of years, since the stone and bronze ages, with fluctuating prosperity and a slow advance. The aboriginal inhabitants of Scandinavia were of unknown racial stock, but it was later invaded by a Germanic people, a branch of the great Indoeuropean stem that spread across Europe and Asia in the last centuries before Christ.

The ancient Romans came into contact with the Germanic tribes of the south on the borders of the Empire, beyond the rivers Rhine and Danube. These southern tribes had certain customs in common and spoke various dialects of the same language. They had long since emerged from the herdsman stage to form a number of kingdoms with some kind of organisation and social structure, but their participation in the classical Mediterranean culture had been small. They had no written literature; the characteristic Germanic runes were used almost exclusively for inscriptions on objects, and later on gravestones.

In the eyes of the Romans with their richer culture and more developed social system these tribes were no better than semi-savage barbarians. Roman historical works made frequent reference to these people, while Tacitus devoted to them a special book which is our chief source of information on them in the first centuries of our era. But this comes from a foreign and hostile nation with no overall knowledge of their culture and customs. Shortly before the end of the 8th century the Northmen make their first definite appearance in written records — and then in the records of other nations, for they were themselves as yet without the art of letters, apart from the runes already mentioned. But they were skilled in other arts and their technical and military development was advanced. The Scandinavian peninsula is mountainous and inaccessible, while the enormous length of coast with its deep fjords and excellent harbours is an invitation to seamen, and at this period the Scandinavians were better shipwrights and sailors than any in Europe. They were tough and aggressive, well equipped with defensive armour, could propel missiles, both spear and arrow, at long ranges, while in close combat they used long-handled axes, considered the most terrible of weapons. When their homelands became overcrowded and the wanderlust seized them, they put out in their ships and at first sailed the short distance across the North Sea. In the year 793 they appeared on the isle of Lindisfarne off the coast of Northumberland, site of the monastery of St. Cuthbert and one of the main centres of the English Church. The monks were completely defenceless. They were cut down in an instant by the raiders and the treasures of their monastery plundered. Sea-warriors of this description were called vikings and the age now beginning is named after them. The raid on Lindisfarne was one of those that marked the opening of the Viking Age. News of this easily-won wealth doubtless travelled like wildfire all over Scandinavia. In the succeeding years one raid followed another. The Danes and Norwegians sailed westwards, with the lie of the land: to England, Scotland and Ireland, and even all the way south to France and the Mediterranean. The Swedes went by what was known as the East Way, harrying the countries to the south and east of the Baltic. Soon the vikings were no longer content just

Page from the Book of Icelanders of Ari the Learned. A copy by the Rev. Jón Erlendsson (d. 1672) made from much earlier vellum book, since lost the margins and between the lines there are variants of another copy Jón Erlendsson in the hand of Arni Magnússon.
In the middle of the page we find: Althing was established with the counsel of Úlfljót and all the people the land where it now is, but befor that there was a thing at Kjalarnes which Thorstein, son of Ingolf the Settler and father of Thorkel Moon lawspeaker, had there, and those chieftains that attended it."
Arnamagnean Collection, Copenhagen No. 113 b, fol: Íslendingabók, 17th century.

auka

Vlfliotz log kolloþ. Han var faþ Gunars er
Diuppdæler e Comner frä i Cnafirþi; En þar
v fleſt ſett at þvi ſem þa v Golaþiŋſ log eþa
roþ þlærfs ens Spaka Hozþa Caraſ. v til hvar viþ
ſcyllbi avca eþa af nema, eþa aŋaŋ veg ſetia.

Vlfliotr var avſtr i Löm. En ſva er ſagt at Emr
Beitſtor væri foſtbroþ haŋ ſa er kaŋaþi Iſland alt
at raþi haŋ aþr Alþiŋi væri att. en honom fecc
hvr maþr pening til a landi her. En þ gaf ſe þat ſiþ
til Hofa.

hic minoris secti-
onis indiciū n̄
vero capitis, in
altero exempl.

Alþiŋi vaſ ſett at raþi Vlfliotz oc allra lanz
maŋa þar er nv eſ. En aþr vas þiŋ a Kiala
neſi þat eſ þorſteiŋ iŋolfſ ſ lannama maŋz faþ
þorkels mana Logſogo maŋs hafþi þar oc hofþiŋi
þir eſ at þvi hvrfv. En maþr hafþi ſecr orþit af
þreſs morþ eþa leyſiŋſ ſa er land atti i Blaſcogo
þ eſ nefndr þorer Croppinſkeggi. En dottor ſonr
þs eſ callaþr þorvalldr Croppinſkeggi. ſa eſ for ſiþ
i Auſtfiorþo. oc brendi þar iŋi Gunar broþor ſiŋ.

Sva ſagþi Hallur Orækiaſ. En ſa het Kolur eſ
myrdr vaſ. viþ þ eſ kend gea ſo eſ þar eſ kolloþ
ſiþan Cols gea ſem hraŋ furþufc. Land þ varþ
Allzheriar fe. En þ logþo lanðz meŋ til Alþiŋis
ŋ ajzlo. Af þvi eſ þar Almeŋiŋ at viþa til alþiŋis
i Scogom. oc a heiþom hagi til Hroſa hafnar. þ
ſagþi Vlfheþiŋ oſſ.

allt
bropor
siþan

to raid the coasts for plunder or occupy outlying headlands. They began to ravage inland, mustered great viking hosts, conquered whole provinces and established independent viking states.

Thus for a considerable period the Danes controlled all Northeastern England in the area known as the Danelaw, while the Norwegians conquered parts of Ireland and founded kingdoms there, securing a permanent hold on Dublin, which was ruled by Norse kings through the greater part of the 10th and 11th centuries. Vikings also sailed up the rivers Loire and Seine and harried the country on both banks. Paris was besieged by vikings for a whole winter, the

Decorated intitial from an ancient manuscript.

Arnamagnean Collection, Copenhagen No. 350, fol: Jónsbók, 14th century

defence of the city being quite widely chronicled. Rouen fell into viking hands and became the capital of the considerable and powerful state known as Normandy because of its origins. Gongu-Hrolf (Rollo), the leader of the Normans, became a count of the king of France in the year 911, and his more famous descendant William Duke of Normandy beat England into permanent subjection at Hastings in the year 1066. On the East Way the Slavs called in the Swedes to aid them against the Mongol tribes that were invading their territory from the east. The Russian *Nestorian Chronicle* records that the first Russian state was founded by Rurik, who was a Swedish viking. Its capital was at Novgorod, known by the Northmen as Holmgard. The viking raids caused an enormous upheaval throughout Europe in their day. To the Scandinavian lands they brought wealth and various cultural

ssign to you my property at . . . on
ch tenure as has been from ancient
es."

the whole dealings between men
peaceful, but when a dispute arises
y are quick to take up the weapons
ich are never far from their hands.
changes settled with weapons were
g thought most worth telling about.
ss is recorded of the other kind: the
-to-day business of the people and
ir obedience to the careful
scriptions of the law.

al Library, Copenhagen, Thott No.
30, fol: Jónsbók, about 1400.

streams. And yet, with a few exceptions, nowhere did the vikings succeed in creating an enduring national state of their own. Though some of their states, such as Normandy and Holmgard, became powerful, the small ruling element was gradually absorbed by the native mass, losing both language and national identity. The only places where this did not happen were previously uninhabited lands occupied by the vikings.

"Iceland was first settled from Norway in the days of Harald Fairhair, son of Halfdan the Black, at the time when Ivar, son of Ragnar Furbreeks, put St. Edmund, king of the English, to death. And this was in the year

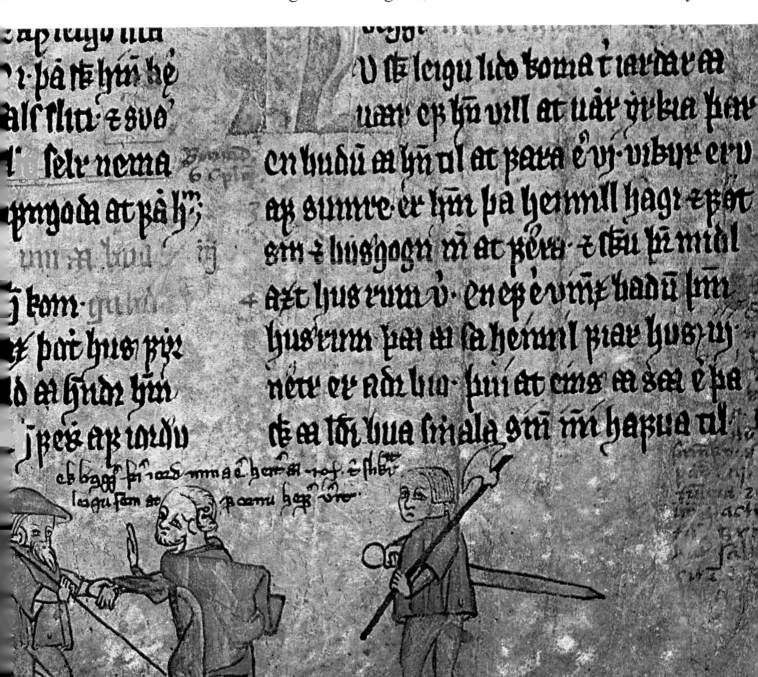

870 after Christ's birth, as is written in his saga.
Ingolf was the name of a Norwegian man who is
truly said to have first gone thence to Iceland when
Harald Fairhair was sixteen years of age, and a
second time a few years later. He settled in the south
at Reykjavik... And wise men have said that in sixty
years all Iceland was settled, and no more after that."
So wrote Ari the Learned in his Book of Icelanders.
The settlement of Iceland shows better than anything
else the great vigour and initiative of the Northmen
in the Viking Age. Thousands of settlers crossed the
stormy seas in open vessels; men with their wives and
children and other kinsfolk, housecarls and thralls.
With them they took clothes and provisions, utensils
and domestic equipment, both indoor and outdoor,
and beside these the necessary livestock: sheep, cattle,
horses, goats, pigs and poultry. This extraordinary
migration reminds one of the marvellous southern
tales of Noah's Ark, in which all mankind and the
whole of animal creation found sanctuary.
The settlement was motivated by the same causes as
the viking raids: overcrowding in the homeland and
an urge for novelty and quick profits. During the
Age of Settlement the climate of Iceland must have
been relatively mild. The immigrants enjoyed all the
advantages of a land untouched and unspoiled by the
hand of man. There was an abundance of fish in the
rivers and lakes and coastal waters of the island. The
lowlands were covered with rich pasture and
birchwood that reached high up the slopes of the
mountains. Some of the newcomers described the
new country as a fishing-station, while one declared
that every blade of grass dripped butter. However, it
was soon found that there were two sides to the
picture and the Icelandic weather could be somewhat
unaccountable. One of the earliest would-be settlers
lost all his livestock in the rigours of the first winter,
and went back. Before leaving he climbed a high
mountain and saw a fjord filled with drift-ice,
whereupon he gave the country its chilly name.
Unwonted events in Norway stimulated the exodus
from that country and speeded up the settlement.

Formely there had been petty kings in every district, but now Harald Fairhair subjugated the land and made himself supreme king. Western Norway was a great breeding-ground of vikings and here it was that Harald met with the stiffest resistance, for he made every effort to pacify the country and destroy their power. After his victory many of his enemies left the land, some sailing to Iceland, and others to the islands of the west across the North Sea where they established bases from which to harry the coasts of Norway. The king then mounted an expedition to the west against the vikings, after which still more of them were driven across to Iceland.

According to the Book of Settlements the majority of the settlers came from the western districts of Norway, especially Sogn and Hordaland. The Icelandic language is closest to the Norwegian dialects originally spoken in these areas. And when the Icelanders adopted a code of law for their commonwealth they based it on the laws of the Gulathing, then in force in Hordaland, Sogn and Fjordene. Thus all the evidence on the origins of the Icelanders points in the same direction.

But from the start the people that settled the new land had a distinctive culture and customs of its own. This may be due to the particular sample of Norwegians that migrated there, and especially to the slight admixture of Celtic stock among the settlers

9

...maug̃ ... hinnun oy eþ ... e þeic þ
hualm̃ eþ sumr er þellar ſlupr a land
lm̃ e adr atte þo ad a anarıs þıoru ko
lm̃ hiuort ꝧ hn̄ vill a ſkıpı edr eykm̃ ...
og haya. Eñ eþ vj ſkynſam̃ m̃ ſana...
eñ nu var talt. þa a ſa ei J þo ad v...
eþ anar a hual. Hn̄ a þegar e hual...
þare þullũ dagleıdum þm̃ er reka a ...
ungs z þı m̃ er hn̄ þar til. þar til er ...
bods m̃. þa ſlu þr rada þm̃ e olꝛo...
reka þa tl þm̃ ord gıora er meſt a J...
ta ꝧ hn̄ eıgı ſialꝼr og abyrgıꝛt vid y...

...egiz̃t. hn e þo no vi luaı
sum̃ ꞇ hual þa a sa hiu:
hn ſꝛ ꞇ birt glyna hua
eyta þar emkıſ nẽa vatz
ꝛ eıdı ad huak ſie vꝛ gellꝛ
ꝛı og abꝛegizt ad aullu /
onñn ad ſenda mañ ſn e̊
d̊bue ſꝛ ſka hual til giord
m̃ bıemꝛ e̊ hꝛ loghgu vn
En eꝛ gleı̊ꝛ m̃ eıga ꝯꝛ
hma tyḫ ſꝛ hñ vardueı
oñum ſmũ. Þu ſk m̃

from the isles of the west. Many of the thralls who later mixed with the freeborn immigrants were also of Celtic origins. Towards the close of the Age of Settlement, about the year 930, the Icelanders combined to establish a common state and general assembly for their land. The constitution of the new commonwealth was unique. The country was divided into four Quarters, and each of these into nine godord, or chieftaincies, except the Northern Quarter, in which there were twelve. The chieftains in charge of the heathen sacrificial rites were called godar, and these were also the leaders of this miniature state. They were of the noblest families among the settlers. In early spring a district assembly would be held in the territory of every three chieftaincies.

The Althing was an assembly of the whole nation, as its name implies. Its sessions lasted two weeks every summer at a time when the sun was highest in the sky and days longest, and were held in magnificent surroundings a little to the east of the homestead of Reykjavik, at a place since known as Thingvöllur — "the vale of the assembly".

Though the Icelandic laws were based on the Norwegian ones of the settlers' native districts, these were considerably supplemented and amended. In their recorded form the laws of the Icelandic commonwealth are far more complex and advanced than any contemporary legal system in neighbouring

The Saga of Eirik the Red tells how Eirik found Greenland, and his son L Vinland the Good. The following account is to be read at the bottom page 96 and top of page 97 in the manuscript: "One day the king (Olaf Tryggvason) spoke to Leif, saying, 'D you mean to go out to Greenland thi summer?' 'That I do,' said Leif, 'if it your will.' The king answers, 'I believ it will be well, and you shall go thith on my errand and announce the Christian faith there.' Leif said it sho be as he would, but this seemed to him a hard errand to carry out in Greenland. The king said that he sav no man better suited to the task tha he – 'and luck will go with you.' 'Onl I have yours,' says Leif. Leif puts ou sea and is long voyaging, and he ma landfall where he had never before expected to find land; there was se sown wheat there, and vines; there were trees of the kind called Maple and of all these they brought some tokens; some timbers so large that they were used for house-building. L found men on a wreck and brought them home with him. In this he showed the greatest nobility and manliness, as in much else, when he brought the Christian faith to the lar and was ever since called Leif the Lucky."

Arnamagnean Collection, Copenhag No. 544, 4to: Hauksbók, beginning the 14th century.

countries. They are preserved complete in two vellum books dating from about the time when the Icelandic national state came to an end, in the latter part of the 13th century, while fragments of other manuscripts also exist. In later times this code of laws came to be known as *Grágás,* or "grey goose".

At the Althing, as might be supposed, the godar were supreme. They were self-appointed members of the legislature *(lögrétta),* the court that amended old laws, drafted new ones and gave judgment on points of law. To ensure its efficient and impartial operation, however, every godi had two advisers, one sitting behind him and one before.

The judicial courts of the Althing were four in number, one for each Quarter. The godar nominated a man each in every Quarter Court, thus giving them effective control, though the interests of parties to a dispute were safeguarded by their right to object to any member of the court on grounds of unsuitability for his office.

Many features of the Icelandic constitution were unique, beside being more democratic than in neighbouring lands. There was no king to oppress his subjects with tyrannical commands. The power was equally divided between thirty-nine farmer-chieftains, among whose tasks was the duty of protecting the interests of their people, each in his own district. The legislative and judicial powers were completely separate and allotted to independent bodies. In criminal cases juries were very much used as evidence of character, the members giving their verdict according to conscience. At a fairly early date a Fifth Court was introduced as a kind of supreme court of appeal for the whole country. Among its other functions this court decided cases that could not be settled in the Quarter Courts. With this, Iceland possessed a three-stage system of justice, as in any advanced modern society: the district court of the spring assembly, and the Quarter and Fifth Courts of the Althing.

The merits of this original and well-devised system were proved both by its duration and results. The

13

Icelandic commonwealth lasted for next to three and
a half centuries, and under its wing there blossomed
a culture whose like was not to be found anywhere
else in Northern Europe. In the latter part of the Age
of the Republic Icelanders were unequalled in some
branches of literature.

In the early centuries after the settlement the
inhabitants possessed a large and effective fleet of
ships, and the wanderlust that had driven their
forefathers to Iceland was still in their blood. From
here they voyaged further westwards in search of
new lands. Eirik the Red, a man from the west of
Iceland, discovered a large country which he named

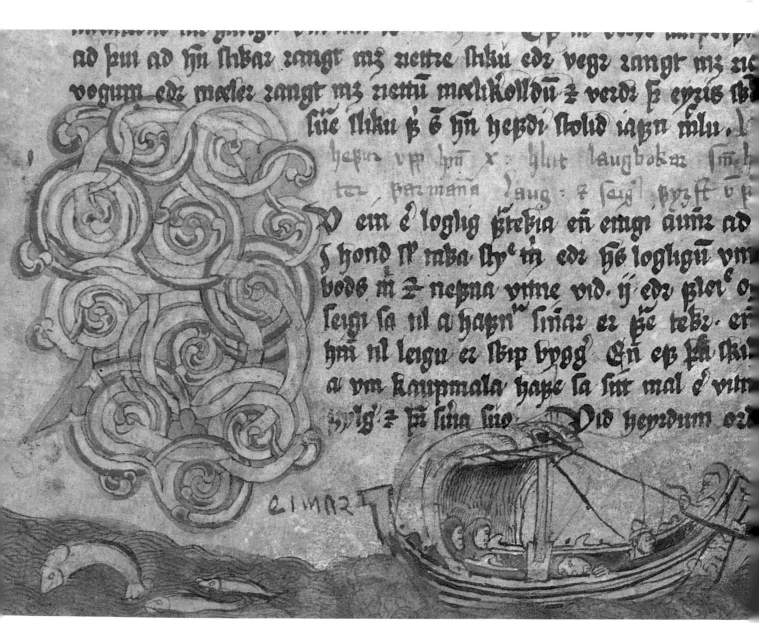

Greenland — "and said that it would urge men to go there, that the land had a good name", observes Ari the Learned. Nor was Eirik disappointed. During the next few years many emigrated from Iceland to Greenland, establishing there a settlement that flourished at the start. From Greenland it was not far to the North American continent, and the sea-dogs of Greenland soon had a glimpse of yet other lands to the southwest. Leif the Lucky, son of Eirik the Red, set out to find these lands about the year 1000, discovering three, to which he gave the names *Helluland* ("flagstone-land"), *Markland* ("forest-land") and Vinland ("wine-land"). *Helluland* and *Markland*

...cient viking ships have been found ...a reasonable state of preservation, ...th on land and under the sea, in ...rway and Denmark. Replicas have ...oved what seaworthy vessels these ...re. Stylized drawings in Icelandic ...nuscripts show how the shape of ...se ships was preserved for ...nturies.

...t: Arnamagnean Collection, No. 345, ...Jónsbók, 16th century. Right: Royal ...rary, Old Collection, No. 3269 a, ...: Jónsbók, 14th century; both ...penhagen.

were probably Baffinland and the Labrador peninsula. *Vinland* could have been Newfoundland, on whose nothernmost promontory very ancient Norse remains have recently been discovered. Thorfinn Karlsefni tried to settle in *Vinland,* but was compelled by the hostility of the natives to leave. To *Markland,* on the other hand, voyages from Greenland continued at least to about the middle of the 14th century.

Greenland followed its mother-country, Iceland, under the rule of Norwegian and later Danish kings. With the passing of the years came a decline in prosperity from deterioration of climate and foreign misrule. The number of seaworthy vessels dwindled and both countries lacked the timber to replace them. The Greenlanders became totally dependent upon the whims of foreign merchants. The Danish authorities neglected Greenland lamentably, and then lost it for about three hundred years.

When explorers rediscovered it at the beginning of the 18th century, they found only the ruins of farms, and poor wooden crosses over the bones of the sea-warriors of old who had discovered America five centuries before the days of Columbus.

The map of Sigurd Stefánsson, schoolmaster at Skálholt, from the of the 16th century. Its model would have been a world map of the type published in 1569 by Gerhard Mercator, supplemented from information about the western hemisphere in old Icelandic writings but moulded by the vague ideas of of the 16th century who had lost contact with the western lands. Am other names on the map are *Grönlandia, Helleland, Marckland, Skrælingeland* (land of the savages and *Promontorium Vinlandiæ.*

The original map has not survived, this is reproduced from Gronlandia Antiqua, by Torfæus (published 170

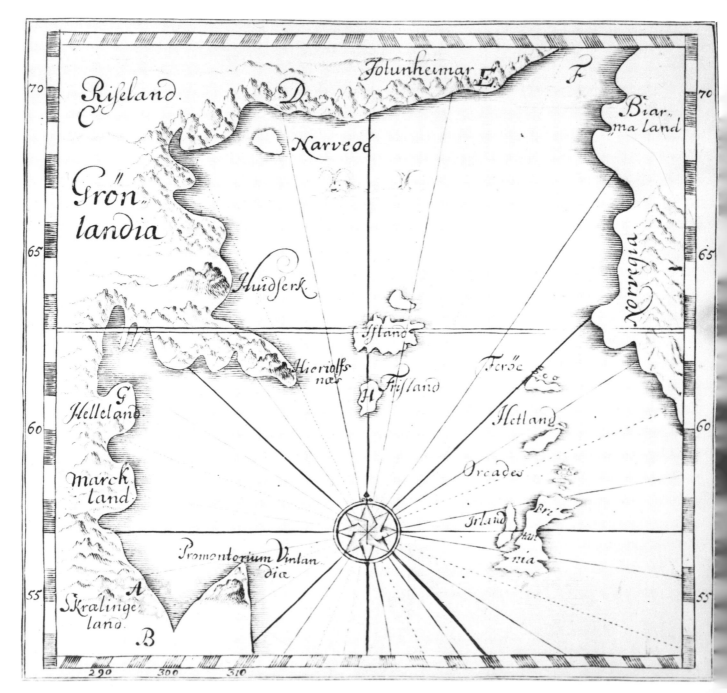

Gods and Heroes

Skallagrimsson. His expression
n in the palace of King Athelstan
ngland is described, while the
d-brimmed hat was worn by him at
.

amagnean Collection, Copenhagen,
426, fol: Sagas of Icelanders, 17th
ury.

In the earliest period the Icelanders had no written
literature. Even the intricate laws of the republic
were transmitted orally from one generation to the
next. It was the office of a special "lawspeaker" to
recite the laws at the Althing, the whole recital
taking three sessions. Nevertheless in this period
there was a rich oral heritage of poetry and story.
Later, in the so-called Age of Writing, the poems and
verses were written down verbatim in their oral form,
while the stories were recorded by creative writers
who combined foreign book-learning with their
native narrative skill. Thus ancestral memories were
both perpetuated and immortalized.

The earliest Icelandic poetry is closely bound up with
heathen beliefs. Many of the ancient poems deal
directly with the old gods, while poetry itself is the
gift of Odin and its language derived from heathen
religion and the legends of the gods. One word has
become a kind of common denominator for these
two, religion and poetry, and this is the name *Edda*.
In fact there are two Eddas: one correctly ascribed to
Snorri Sturluson, the other for a time wrongly
ascribed to Sæmund Sigfusson the Learned (d.1133).
The word *edda* means great-grandmother, but why
this name should have been given to Snorri's learned
work on the ancient art of poetry remains a mystery.
To explain the art of poetry or teach would-be poets
how to compose could not be done without giving an

account of the old beliefs and telling the stories of
the gods on which the poetic vocabulary was based.
Thus Snorri's Edda became not only a handbook for
poets, but also a main source-book on the old
religion.

The first section of Snorri's Edda is called
Gylfaginning. It tells of King Gylfi, who, travelling
incognito under the pseudonym Gangleri ("the weary
walker"), comes all the way to Valholl where he is
enlightened by conversations with the masters of the
hall. In an attractive illustration in one of the
manuscripts of Snorri's Edda at the University
Library of Uppsala Gangleri is shown standing and
listening to the words of the triune person of Odin.
By the dialogue method, adopted from foreign
mediæval didactic works, Snorri achieves a twofold
object: he makes the information fresh and living,
and at the same time places on his puppet-characters
his own responsibility as an orthodox Christian in
dealing with such godless lore.

In Snorri's Edda the world-view of the old Norse
religion is presented. The gods live in Asgard as a
large family, though each individual has his specific
dwelling. Their chief is Odin, god of poetry, runes
and magic. To Valholl, his abode, go all men who
have died in battle. Each day they practise their
favourite sport of killing one another, though every
evening they all rise up unhurt and sit down to drink
together. Many of the principal gods are sons of
Odin. Of these the most popular is Thor, who is also
the biggest and strongest. He batters the giants with
his hammer Mjolnir ("the crusher"), which becomes
the sacred symbol of heathens. Tyr is the god of war.
He is one-handed, having lost a hand which he had
placed as a pledge in the jaws of the wolf Fenrir.
Heimdall is the sentinel of the gods. He sees as well
by night as by day and can hear the grass and the
wool of sheep growing. Baldur is the best of all the
gods. "He is so fair of countenance and so bright that
he shines". But Loki, crafty and the scandal-monger
of the gods, brings about the death of Baldur, who
then descends to the abode of Hel to share a

Völuspá gives vivid glimpses of the
world-picture of heathendom. Here
have the approach of Doomsday, a
may be read in the bottom lines of
second page:
"Garm bays loud
at the cave of the cliff;
bonds will burst
and the wolf run free.
Much lore she knows
and can see further

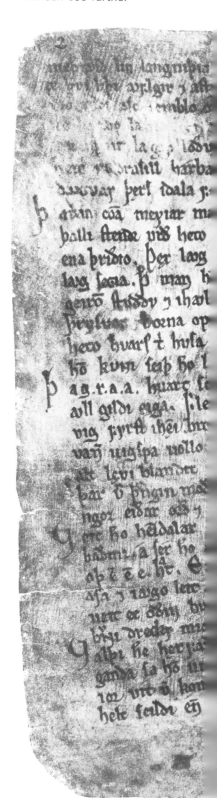

e fate of gods,
e mighty in battle. . .

yal Library, Copenhagen, Old
llection, No. 2365, 4to: Codex
gius manuscript of the Eddic Poems,
th century.

miserable existence with those who die of disease and old age. Njord, the god of navigation, belongs to another race called Vanir. His children are Frey and Freyja, deities of love and fertility who enjoyed an extensive cult throughout Scandinavia.

The gods are at perpetual war with their enemies the giants, who live in the rocks and caves of Jotunheim. With them are associated various monsters such as

Hermód til Heliar reÿd: Rana þann
na strondu, Hvórgi stybur hesti a Isbe
hleipti ad Uutz Kiaptinum.
Þo Helia þarfa hefdi þau, hiulu sự
tum Daudanz Mocb, Hermódᵘ eÿ hra
van, Kalþ blaalita þenan Skrock.
Les XLIII. Eddu, dæmi

Balldur hin Gódi

Hun
gur
dẛ

Sulltu
Knÿfur

the wolf Fenrir, whom the gods bound, and Midgardsorm, the World Serpent, that lies encircling the earth with its tail in its mouth. Thor holds the giants at bay with his hammer for a long time, until they unite in a mighty campaign against the gods. This great Armageddon ends with the death of most of the gods and the destruction of the world by fire by the giant Surt. This is Ragnarok, the twilight of the gods. But after the day of doom the earth will rise up again, ever-green, from the ocean and those gods and men who have survived will live on in the lands of their fathers.

The narrative in Snorri's Edda is based for the most

part on old lays about the gods. But the poems are to some extent discordant, while other fragmentary sources from heathen times on the old religious beliefs are either contradictory or laconic and difficult to interpret.

We have to accept the fact that our knowledge of the ancient religion of heathendom is fragmentary and imperfect. But this is no reason for supposing that it must have been relatively primitive or crude. It should be remembered that direct sources on the heathen beliefs were not recorded to any degree until two centuries after the adoption of Christianity in Iceland. Between lay a number of generations of *presumed* hostility towards the heathen heresies. But the Icelanders' acceptance of the Christian faith was not of a kind to exclude the survival of some heathen concepts and religious attitudes. This may be seen, for example, in a comparison between heathen poems such as *Hávamál* and the heroic lays of the elder Edda on the one hand, and the Sagas of Icelanders, written long after the advent of Christianity, on the other. In both of these literary genres the same ideas prevail, the same obligations and superstitions are found.

It was on the ancient heathen foundations of the Icelandic commonwealth that the national culture of Christian times arose, and in the old sagas heathendom is rescued from oblivion, refined in the crucible of Christianity and revived for endless posterity. Snorri's Edda was used as a textbook for poets, and thus always available in a large number of copies. The oldest surviving manuscript came into the possession of a 17th century bishop of Skalholt, Brynjolf Sveinsson, a great scholar and collector of ancient writings. He presented it to the king of Denmark and like other Icelandic vellum books it is now in the Royal Library in Copenhagen. Another Eddic manuscript is in the Arnamagnean Library, a third in the University Library at Uppsala, as mentioned above, and a fourth in Utrecht, Holland. In all there are some dozens of manuscripts of Snorri's Edda, mostly paper copies of later centuries.

The first writing in the Icelandic tor of which anything certain is known that of the ancient laws of the repu known as Grágás. This was started the winter of 1117-18 at Breidaból Vesturhóp, in the north of Iceland. These laws have been preserved in complete vellum books from the 1? century, beside fragments of other ancient manuscripts.

Arnamagnean Collection, Copenha⟨ No. 334, fol: Grágás (Stadarhólsbó 13th century.

A popular belief grew up that Snorri's Edda was just a summary of an earlier and more substantial Edda by Sæmund the Learncd. Bishop Brynjolf discovered an old vellum book containing most of the poems quoted by Snorri and concluded that this must have been the Edda of Sæmund. He deemed it proper that the two Eddas should share the same fate, and so the latter also ended up in the Royal Library in Copenhagen. It has since long been realised that Sæmund had no part in these poems, most of which date from well before his time. We therefore no longer talk about Sæmund's Edda, but refer to these poems as the Eddic poems, or the Elder Edda. There

is no more precious manuscript than this so-called Codex Regius which contains many of the finest jewels of old Icelandic — and indeed all ancient Germanic — literature. The first of these is *Völuspá*, and next after it, *Hávamál*, the great moral poem of the Viking Age. In *Hávamál* speaks the poet of the new land who has travelled far and wide and experienced much; made friends and enjoyed life —

though in moderation. The human wisdom acquired by men through travel and experience is the supreme virtue. But even wisdom should be in moderation:

Wise within bounds
let each man be;
never too wise by far —

The poem is informed by the optimism of the pioneer; an ode to work, the joy of life, and friendship:

Young was I once
and walked alone,
then wandered far from the way.
Rich I felt
when a friend I found;
man is a man's delight.

No living man is so wretched that there is no profit in him, but after death all is useless. Yet one thing endures:

"The World-serpent gaped at the ox-head, and the hook fastened in the of the serpent. . . No man has seen fearful sights that might not see wh Thor fixed the serpent with his eye the serpent stared back from above him and spewed poison." So Snorri his Edda. Thor goes out fishing with the giant Hymir. Hymir catches two whales, but Thor fishes for the Worl serpent with the head of an ox for b Having drawn the serpent to the surface, though, he loses it when th terrified giant cuts the line. Thor throws his hammer, Mjölnir, after th serpent, but misses, and the monste lies encircling the ocean until Doomsday.

Arnamagnean Collection, Copenhage No. 738, 4to, 17th century.

Flocks will die
and kinsfolk die
and a man himself the same,
but a good name
will never die
for the one who wins himself fame.

The later part of Codex Regius contains poems about ancient Germanic heroes. Some of these are known from the age of the migration of nations, for example Atli (Attila) king of the Huns and Jormunrek (Eormenric) king of the East Goths. Others are unidentifiable in earthly reality, though they are presented as the greatest of kings: Sigurd who slew the dragon Fafnir and rode through flames to the hall of Brynhild — he also appears in the German Nibelungenlied — and his brother Helgi Hunding's Bane who revisited his love from Valholl and held her alive one night in his cold arms.

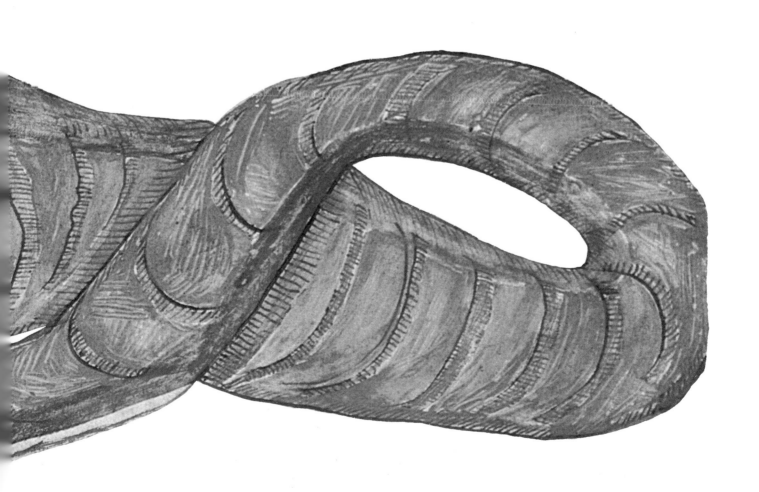

The material of the heroic lays is invariably tragic. All is dominated by the concept of honour, hard and merciless. The hero is in duty bound to defend his honour, even at the cost of his life or by deeds of cruelty. Hogni Gjukason does not flinch, though his heart is cut from his living body. Gunnar plays his harp in the serpents' den until the adder strikes him dead. Never will they reveal where the gold of Fafnir is hidden:

Swift Rhine shall hold
the heroes' strife-mint,
god-begotten
hoard of Niflungs;
in weltering water
shall the foreign rings gleam,
sooner than gold
on the hands of the Huns.

The Eddic poems were composed in a metre which in early ages was common to all Germanic peoples. Instead of the end-rhyme and regular rhythm familiar in the verse of later times, it was characterised by alliteration and an irregular pattern of stress on the principal word in each line. This metrical form is also found in Old German and Old English heroic poetry (Lay of Hildebrand, Beowulf). But Icelanders also composed other verses, of a type quite different from the Eddic poems, both in form and content. These were the so-called scaldic poems. This type of poetry was of Scandinavian origin and reached its full maturity in Iceland. Scaldic verse is characterised by a very elaborate form with a special poetic diction and a complex arrangement of words and sentences. By content, there are two main groups: eulogistic poems (especially addressed to kings) and occasional verses. When young Icelanders travelled abroad they would present themselves before the king of the country and recite a poem in his honour, receiving their reward both in gifts and honours. In the second place, the scald improvised verses on various occasions: on journeys by land and sea; occasions of joy and sorrow. Battles and slayings

"Five hundred doors
and forty more
I wit in Valhöll be.
Eight hundred heroes
march abreast through one,
when to war with the wolf they wen

Arnamagnean Collection, Copenhag
No. 738, 4to, 17th century. The ver
is from Grímnismál in the Poetic Ed

are one of the favourite themes, and as might be supposed these poets could also describe their tribulations in affairs of the heart. Such verses were never collected in a single manuscript like the Eddic lays, but have been preserved as an element in the sagas: the poems of eulogy in the Sagas of Kings and the occasional verses in the Sagas of Icelanders.

The greatest scaldic poet of all was Egil Skallagrimsson, who lived in the 10th century and was the son of a leading settler and a chief in his own country. A special saga was written about him. Whatever its accuracy or historical value, this is a major work of art. In his childhood Egil looks forward with eager anticipation to the years of manhood in a verse which demonstrates the warlike spirit that was bred in the bone among vikings.

He had his wish. He sailed to foreign lands, turned viking and composed poems in honour of powerful kings. On his voyages and battles he made a host of occasional verses packed with vivid imagery. But his greatest fame as a poet is for two poems composed in a simple metre: one for the friend who came to his aid in the hour of need; the other for his two sons, lost in tragic circumstances. One *(Arinbjarnarkvida)* is only found in the manuscript compilation of Sagas of Icelanders known as *Mödruvallabók,* where it is written on the reverse side of a leaf of Egils Saga. This one page is only half legible, however, and the conclusion of the poem would have been on the following leaf, which is lost. The second *(Sonatorrek)* has had similar rough treatment. Granted it is complete, but only in later paper manuscripts with a very corrupt text. Yet there is enough of both poems left undamaged to afford us an impressive glimpse of this poet, the first designated Icelander to appear in self-portrait. The poems are at one and the same time infused with the warmth of personal feeling and tempered with manly strength and verbal magic. We take no offence though he regards his work with the self-assurance of a Horace in the last stanza of *Arinbjarnarkvida,* which, thanks to a merciful providence, is preserved in Snorri's Edda.

The saga tells how, when he has news of the drowning of his son Bodvar, Egil makes up his mind to starve himself to death, but his daughter talks him into living until he has composed an elegy. In the poem there is a violent attack on the divine powers, Odin and the sea-god Ægir, that have robbed him of his sons. Once he had been on good terms with Odin, giver of victory and god of poetry, but now this former friend has betrayed his trust. As the poem progresses, however, Egil's spirits revive, and finally he triumphs over his grief, having forged a recon-ciliation with the gods in the act of composition.

Quill-pen and Parchment

Books came to Iceland with the Christian faith, adopted by the Althing in the year 1000 — books in Latin; the sacred writings of the Catholic Church, written on parchment. The priests of the new faith all needed books for the performance of the liturgy. Not unnaturally, it was some time before Christianity took firm root. The first Icelandic bishop appeared just after the middle of the 11th century with his see at Skalholt in the south. Half a century later a second diocese was established at Holar in the north. These two sees were to be the main educational centres of the country until the late 18th century, when Reykjavik emerged as a capital. Cathedral schools for the training of men for the priesthood operated at both sees, almost without a break, up to this time.

Just as the political structure of the Icelandic state was unique, so did the position of the Church there differ from that in other countries at the time. Christian chieftains replaced the heathen temples on their estates by churches. At first the priests were foreigners, but later it became common for the sons of chieftains to be trained for the priesthood and take orders, and if the owner of the church was not ordained, he would have a cleric in his service, but control the church and its finances himself. Thus from the beginning the Church in Iceland was subject to lay control and not, as elsewhere, a

29

virtually independent state within the state. This had two consequences: first, the Church acquired a national character, and second, the lay chieftains became literate. Add to this the fact that the Icelanders possessed an immense store of unwritten poems and stories and a complicated law full of detailed provisions that cried out to be recorded in writing, and it is not difficult to see why the evolution of learning and literature in Iceland should have taken a course very different from that found in other Christian countries. Elsewhere men of learning were a class apart, enclosed within the walls of their churches and monasteries. Their literary language

was mainly Latin and their writings mostly of a Christian and devotional flavour. But in Iceland men of learning had their feet firmly planted in the secular world and were informed with both knowledge and love of the national, Icelandic, lore. Thus the art of writing was soon taken into the service of native culture. Almost all Icelandic authors wrote in their native tongue, and not in Latin. Religious works were both translated, and composed in Icelandic, and other foreign studies accorded the same treatment. Most important of all, though — in Iceland a completely native literature of considerable

volume and outstanding quality was created.

The production of books was not confined to centres of learning, but was carried on in farmhouses all over the country. The most famous Icelandic author was Snorri Sturluson, a layman, and the most famous manuscript, *Flateyjarbók,* was written in a farmhouse in the north. From the earliest times literacy was general, and continued to be so down to the present day. Even the monasteries were more secular in tone than elsewhere, being recruited to some extent from the ranks of elderly farmer-chieftains who sought in them a haven after the storms of life.

Icelandic scholars of this period were in direct contact with the principal centres of learning throughout Christendom. At the beginning, the main source of Christian lore was England, a country with which there were long and various links. The first bishops of Skalholt, Isleif and his son Gizur, both studied in Germany, while Sæmund the Learned, Gizur's closest collaborator, spent years of study in France. The two Icelandic sees were at first subject to the archdiocese of Bremen; later to Lund in Scania, and finally, from 1153, to Trondheim in Norway. But although the scholarly links were strongest with Scandinavia in the years of its Christian culture, direct ties between Icelanders, both students and other travellers, and the British Isles and the Continent were never broken. This helps to explain the great variety and fertility of the old Icelandic literature.

The earliest work known to have been recorded in writing in the Icelandic language was the law of the ancient commonwealth, which was in urgent need of transcription. The writing down of the laws began about 1100. This prepared the way for native literature, just as the Bible did in other countries. However, religious works, some translated from the Latin, were also among the first writings in the vernacular. Soon men began to compose Icelandic historical and other learned works. At the beginning these were all dry and scrupulous in their pursuit of

31

truth and accuracy, but later came the writing of sagas in which the emphasis was on the art of the storyteller and entertainment went hand-in-hand with edification.

The first Latin books soon required replacing and each new cleric needed his own books. The demand increased still more with the advent of vernacular literature. Icelandic literary culture created a demand for Icelandic book production. In this period the making of books in Europe depended almost exclusively on the use of various kinds of skin. The Icelanders invariably used calfskin. Yet another possible factor in the great literary activity of the Icelandic people was the special suitability of their country for cattle-breeding. The large supply of calves offered itself, as it were, to be used as the raw material for books.

The hide had first to be shaved with a sharp knife. This was a skilled task, for the surface must not be hairy, while the skin must on no account be cut. Yet it is not uncommon to find cuts in vellum leaves, and here the scribe jumps over the gap, even though it comes in the middle of a word. Points of greyish-coloured calf's hair can sometimes be seen on the edges of these gaps. When the hide had been shaved,

The Bible was probably never translated as a whole in Catholic tim but the earlier part of the Old Testament, up to the end of the second book of Kings, exists in anc manuscripts. The translation of different parts is of varying periods provenance, but has been combine transcripts under the title *Stjórn* – reference being to God's rule over world. The first (and latest) part is much expanded with comments fro various mediæval works. Some manuscripts of Stjórn are beautifull decorated, as may be seen here. O the left we see Adam and Eve rega themselves on the fruit of the Tree Knowledge, while the serpent coils about the trunk of the tree. On the right Abraham is on the point of sacrificing his son Isaac when the angel of the Lord catches hold of t sword and prevents the blow.

Arnamagnean Collection, Copenhag No. 227, fol: Stjórn, 14th century.

het kambises þeckir vasto yf egipta lði al. xv. ar
stalp hins rikis er seti ap þra riki alltr idagha all
uerr kgs er oðin napni het at tarreris. Seruch
gat nachor þan tima sem hn var primgr en þ upp
hafa anars heims alltra noru liðin. c. rr. ok iij. ar
at so dogum hofe sotka riki tanar riki siritoni
orum. Nathor gat tharam eðr thare þan tima s
en hn hapði. rr. ar ok xx. en az oðum heims alt
ri uer liðin. cc. i ij ar ok xx. Æ dogþum thare
histradiz anar heimsin alltr z sem hn var hau
ugr at asto. hapandi ept æ ebrelstra masla tali
cc. ar at lx. nigþt z iij. ar. En eptr þgu lxx. mð
precum snilpundar siautighi ok ij. ar. þ upp

ha þa z mprona
abraham z huer
su hafi gekk ut
az challdea. Gene
sis. captulum.

thare gat þria
sþin. abram. na
chor. ok aram.
þan tima sem h
var ner hautig
t at aldri. Ara
var ellztr þrig
gt sþin sueha. nachor þar nest en abram yngs
tr. aram gat at eiga þessu. iij liþm. loth z res
tham saraý ok nischam z andaðiz isuri bg isu
mu eignu þostr sin challdea sem nu þetr at sa
panda þelr smum thare ok þar iar daþr. þer
bue dnir abram z nachor þeingu ser hstr spur
gelts abram með þelu smum ok athans raði
ar eigsa brodur dottur sina saraý. en abha na
chor þla þyriegnda brodur dottur sina melch
am voru þer bsdar dætr aram ok sýstr lothz
sem þyr var saght. en azþinat saraý var uþyri
a z arru eingi liþm u bonda snu abram þa rok
hn loth brodur hsnar z brodur sun sin seer z oltz
bernis ok serisumar stad. Stolast hystr. Chall
dei slogbu þan mstratui mat ar sr þyrkabu el
lð. en eckrn er upp a þra tungu vmsun er sn
þurun eðr leiddir skiotlegha z serilegha srn þþar
z sem með þerma þeru þan skradi eptr þui
sem segir. En z þan skysto at sþir thare z sialpr

hafi victon meðrengu mon estorn þyrka. þa sy
stendu kallder sin þiemu alham z aram leidom
utan veggi z miskonu z eo aram þar ept þin sen
sm jnn segra ertaþam þralistaðir þar az meðqu
de miskon z þustrngi huadan az erst er sleit ok
sungit az þin ar gað leystr han ok studd ut az þi
challdeorum. Huz þa sok at thare z rnsu az ssha
ttar dauda z diapisons
smaraguan z þsi þottre æ miga þiola þer morgio
der z meinseir sem challders uenn þsn til þat han
þyrkaðsi þa heldr en aðr ellorn þa tok hafi þar
rad at þin stolsk iðaur oz challder z hapði með
ser sun sren abram ok loth sun sin sem nu sin aras
z smar konu sina saraý hsispru abram z thyr
adis smu foð utra challdea lðr til sos lðe se þann
tima byggbu kynsrun z apkiem charams z þa
hetr sua tharaan. En sidam var kassat idea ok ko
rm isuan stad eðr dg imesopotamiea lor se hettr
aram en sun kostrburo thare z setru þar sina hy
gd s sem ymnisega er tarrpat z sagt. oreð eðr cho
ren z tarian stad ras eðr rasan z seru sina hy
gd tharram z andadtr thare þar s sem h haþ
ði. cc. uema z v. ar. Speolm hyst. Hns sem all
er ackier uerasto ar nun uisto z uo þdiz i þhan
var skindþuda uisto z uatren seþþyr var þ saght
þa var siesi az aðram mærri skola snu skapiara
z snsta þ með snu skyrnsend az snmu urngla
iskpan z suornu gang með snu at sþi var hn
beeti astrologus at aller sual þorpabir z svomað
rz az þans skipan ok þorsio. tonguim nim m
nur þaþsi sþn þar z þnllskomma z aliqmleyha
æ stundan huar þ er eingr gnd nnraðiz sþn ok
lærdi sþn en mnlkli þmærri z þuslulleyhar az
sþn suemu sem aldi haþsu sþn az snni hist z uistor
hskrura skenng eðr sktsumgh. þ snn er abram
gekk ut az aram z byggdr bgmia damaseu
ok kom sidam iмеr ægipta land.

C prru s sem thare uar andaþr z aram
an eðr charram sem þyr uar sagt.
talaði gud s til smar hs abram.
þan tima sem hn uar halþ auur eð at alstri. þa
lsk ut þu abram az þmn þostr þn z eighin þþ
dur leyrd iðaur az þmmin þrnd haga z þmi þþ
dur hus z til bergi ok þar t sr lsr sem ek manty

it was scraped, cleaned and pulled, then pinned out and stretched, and finally kneaded by hand. For the kneading an instrument called *brák* was used. It was usually made of horn, in the shape of a ring or horseshoe. The skin was twisted together and pulled backwards and forwards through the *brák,* until it was smooth, soft and pliable. It was now true parchment, in colour, thickness and appearance not unlike high quality paper, but softer and stronger. The parchment was now cut into rectangular sheets of varying sizes, according to the fold intended for the book (folio, quarto, etc.). In the largest books there was only a single broadsheet from each calfskin when all the edges had been trimmed off. The sheet was then folded in the middle to form two leaves (folio). If two sheets, or four leaves, were cut from each skin, we get a four-leaf fold (quarto, or 4to.). These four leaves could then be folded again across the middle to give an eight-leaf fold (octavo, or 8vo.). The folded sheets were arranged in order in groups, generally of eight leaves each, corresponding to what are known as quires in ordinary printed books. But more was needed before the writing could begin. The composition of the text had to be straight, with parallel edges and straight horizontal lines. This was provided for by scratching small marks at the edge of the page and ruling the columns and lines with a stylus. If the leaves were large the text was generally in double columns, as was later the custom in larger printed books.

Finally we come to the actual lettering. One can scarcely speak of a special class of scribes in Iceland, as in many other countries. However, the ability to write was general, though naturally some copyists were more skilled than others and therefore sometimes employed for a time by some wealthy man who wanted books of his own. The greater part of *Flateyjarbók* was copied by two priests, identified by name, for the landowner Jón Hákonarson.

The writing was always done with a quill-pen, probably usually cut from swans' feathers, though the feathers of smaller birds are also mentioned in this

King Olaf the Saint, with his symbols crown, axe and orb.

Arnamagnean Collection, Copenhagen No. 673 a III, 4to: Book of Drawings, 15th century.

connexion. "With this pen I am well pleased, though it's from a raven" says an old verse. The ink was made by boiling the bear-berry plant (arctostaphylos uva-ursi). It is black and sometimes glossy, and extremely durable. This is just as well, for Icelandic vellum books have had to go through a great deal. When the writing was done the quires were laced together and bound in wooden boards. Holes were pierced in the board and the laces attached to them with pegs. Sometimes the board and back of the volume were covered with dyed and ornamented leather. But Icelandic books were very much read and as the years and centuries went by the bindings

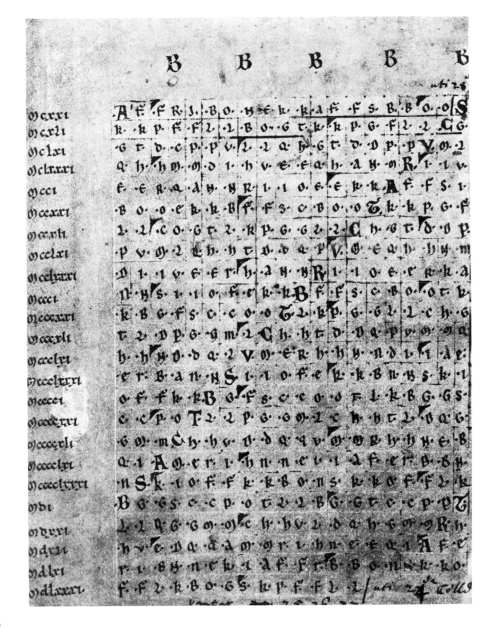

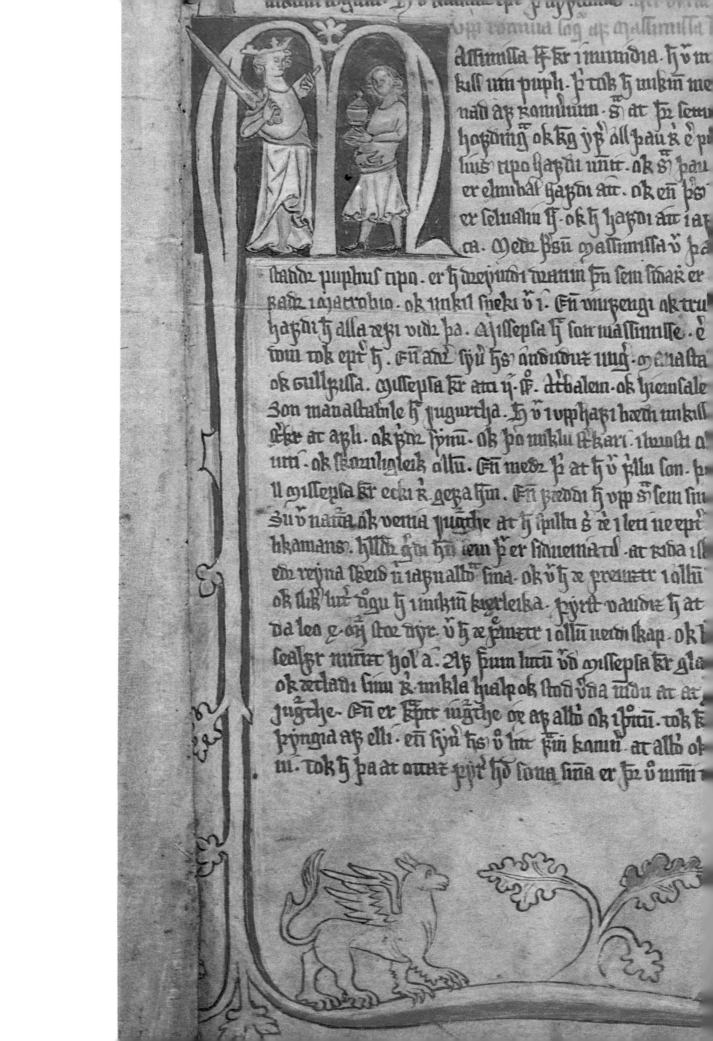

ap oglann. H o ſalann epr Iuguṛ... þer oꝛa
up roınına log az maſſınıſſa l

aſſınıſſa kᷓ kᷓ ı mumıdıa. h v m
kıſſ um þuꝑh. þ tok þ mıkın me
naꝺ az ꝛomuıdum. S at þᷓ ſem
haꝛdıng ok tᷓg ıꝥ all þau ᷓ e pᷓ
luıs ꝛıpo haꝺı umᷓ. ok ꝥ þau
er elmıbal haꝺı ᷓm. ok en þᷓ
er ſeluahu ᷓ. ok h haꝺı ᷓm ıaꝛ
ca. Medᷓ þſu ꝗaſſınıſſa v þa
ſtandᷓ þuphuſ ꝛıpo. er h dᷓeıuuꝛ uaunı þꝛı ſem ſıdaᷓ er
ꝛadᷓ ıaıaꝛꝛobıo. ok mıkıl ſneku v ı. En muꝛꝛengı ok tru
haꝺı þ alla ꝛꝝı uıdᷓ þa. aıſſepſa þ ſon maſſınıſſe. e
toıu tok eptᷓ þ. En adᷓ ſyu hᷓs anduudᷓ ıuug. oꝛ enaſta
ok ꝗuıllꝛuſſa. cyuſſepſa kᷓ atu ij. ſᷓ. ꝛᷓbaleın. ok hıeınſale
Son manaſtatnle þ ıuguꝛtha. h v ıupphatı bꝛꝝtı mıkıll
ꝝꝛ at aꝛꝝ. ok ꝛm ſynu. ok þa mıklu ꝝ̄kaꝛı. ıꝑmıſtı aꝲ
uᷓuı. ok ſkaꝛnlıgleık alltu. En medᷓ þ at h v ꝝllu ſon. þ
ll eyıſſepſa kᷓ eckı ᷓ. geꝛa kᷓın. En bᷓœd_ þ upp ſᷓ ſem ſın
Su v naıuı. ok ueıma þuꝛthe at h ſpıltı ᷓ ꝛꝝ ı leıı ne eptᷓ
lıkamanꝛ. kıldᷓ þ̄u hᷓs ıeıu þ er ſıduemıꝛtıl. at ꝛꝝda ıl
edᷓ ꝛeıına ſkeıd u ıaꝛu alldᷓ ſına. ok v þ ꝛꝝ pᷓœuꝝtt ı allu
ok tıkᷓ luᷓ ꝝgu þ ı mıklu bꝝꝛleıka. þyꝛtı uaudᷓ þ at
da leo. ꝛ oꝛ ſtoᷓ uıyꝛ. v h ꝛꝝ ꝝtuꝝtt ı allu ueın ſkap. ok h
ſealꝛ mıᷓ hol a. Aꝝ ꝗum luıu vd eyıſſepſa kᷓ gla
ok ꝝdladı ſınu ᷓ mıkla hıalp ok ſtod vꝺa uıdu at at
ıuguꝛthe. En er ꝛtᷓ ıuꝛthe. oꝛ aꝝ alldᷓ ok ıꝥuıu. tok ᷓ
ꝛyngıd aꝝ ellı. en ſyu hᷓs v luᷓ þın kamıu. at allᷓ ol
ın. tok þ þa at otuᷓ þꝛ hᷓo ſona ſına er þᷓ v uuıu

Brat v h̄ s̄ kiek puplio. at h̄ kallaði Iugurtham til allz starfs.
en h̄ v̄ buın til allz haſka þs er h̄ viſtði. Iugurtha b̄ mikla at
hyſon þ hu ꝩ̄ mætti þ hellz ga. er ꝛomuꝛn vęri meſte þyr
kr at. Ok þ til ꝼꝺr ꝩ̄ huiki vas ne erꝩn ok ȳ hꝛꝼs haſka. s̄
kom h̄ s̄ ikierleika v̄ hꝺſong ok alla aꝺa ꝛomua. Envm
u̇ þs hrꝛddut h̄ allꝛ meſt. h̄ v̄ hꝩn ſterkaꝛta til uapns. ok
hꝩn ſkiotaꝛtt í arꝛꝛs. en az þ v̄ſaðı puplus Iugurtha þ til
ſem meſt þꝼtı. at h̄ v̄ ꝛꝛuꝛꝛtt. ok h̄ þꝛn at alld v̄nꝩttꝛ
ꝛꝛaði þs ne ꝛtlan v̄ h̄ az þ̄ſu meſt eliſkað az hꝩn ok ꝺꝺltn
hꝛnum. urðu ok s̄ allir at h̄ ꝩ̄m hꝩn mieſtan ſꝺꝛn. h̄ v̄ ok hꝩ
n̄ ꝛuillꝺaꝛtꝛ az þe. ok hꝩn ꝛuillataꝛtꝛ v̄ alla m̄. Fra Romulo
þꝼa tuiua v̄ ih̄ ꝛomꝺia iug ꝛigꝺ m̄ ok ꝺꝛigꝺ þꝛ. ok Iugꝺtho
er metta uirðu uirtugiꝺꝛꝛna en mankoſti. ok v̄ ſtꝛꝼ ok otꝛ
iꝩgg. þꝛ tolðu iaꝛnan þ Iugꝺho ek ꝩꝛſeꝼla ꝼr anꝺaꝺꝛt i m̄
mꝺꝛa at engin vęri iaꝛnual til ꝛallꝛn at ſꝼrꝛꝛꝛ i ꝛikꝛt ſem
Iugꝺtha. ok ꝼꝺgðu h̄ tꝼ alla ꝼurt til at ꝼa þꝩ̄ m̄ ſlikꝛ ꝛikꝛt.
ok uit þꝛt m̄; ſoᷙu at í ꝛoma tꝺg e allꝛr urt ꝼaltꝛ uið ꝼe
en ſiꝺan er uuꝛn v̄ numancia. ſꝼr allr hꝩn apt til ꝛoa
tꝺg. ok at ſkilnadı. ꝛallꝛ puplus apo. Iugꝺhꝛ i ſm̄ atuꝛgı.
ok gaz hꝩn ſtoꝛmanligꝛ ḡꝛꝼ. ok iataðı hꝩn ſin þylgꝺ.
z þyꝛꝼ. ok lꝺꝛaðı h̄ miok þ ꝺllum ꝛoma tꝺg hiꝺ þꝺt er
þ v̄. Siðan leiddı puplꝩ h̄ ꝛꝛ einmꝛlı. ok ꝛeð hꝩn ꝼꝺl
ꝛꝛaꝺ. ok mꝛꝛ s̄. Elſka þu vmattu ꝛomꝺua apꝛ̄m̄liga
en geꝛ þm ꝛ ſtoꝛ gꝼaꝺ ꝛꝼmꝛliga. ok uit þꝛ þ̄ uit at þer
ꝛ gott at kaupa at þam er m̄g eigu. en ek þu uillꝛgo
ꝺu með þꝛu hallꝺat s̄ ſem þu heꝼr aſt ſyꝛt þa er
þ ꝛikꝛ i ꝛꝺꝼ. en ek þu ꝛaſ þ ꝛaꝺ þm. t ꝛeꝩme aſt
v̄ ſeꝺ. Fra Jugurtha ku̇ aꝺꝛaſtr. þa uis þu þe zliþ.

became worn. None of the covering of ancient vellum books has survived, though quite a few wooden boards and fragments of old binding-laces have done so.

The production of vellum books was always very costly. For *Flateyjarbók,* which contains 225 leaves, 113 calfskins were used and a vast amount of work went into the making and writing of it. To save time and parchment the scribes would make great use of abbreviations and symbols for particular words and syllables. This was known as "binding" and the abbreviations were "bonds". In some manuscripts there is scarcely a word written in full. The symbols, many of them of foreign origin, varied somewhat according to the school of copyists and age of the manuscripts, though their common origins can easily be detected.

At the beginning of the Age of Writing an Icelandic phonetician undertook the task of adapting the Latin alphabet to conform with the Icelandic language and to this end compiled a very remarkable work known as the First Grammatical Treatise. This is our basic authority on the Icelandic tongue in the earliest phase of the written language.

When manuscripts were made the writer often left blank spaces for the initial letters of each chapter. Later another, more skilled scribe would add these artistically, often with inks of various colours, decorating and tinting them. In important places he might elaborate the initials with illustrations suitable to the subject-matter, executed in graceful lines and beautiful colours. Many Icelandic manuscripts are beautifully illuminated in this way, and the development of Icelandic pictorial art, with the constant influence of new cultural streams from abroad, may be traced in these pictures and decorations. A comparison between Icelandic vellum books and the mediæval manuscripts to be seen in museums in other countries admittedly shows a considerable difference in the degree of elaboration. The parchment of the foreign exhibits is usually clean and white, often with gold-leaf in the initials,

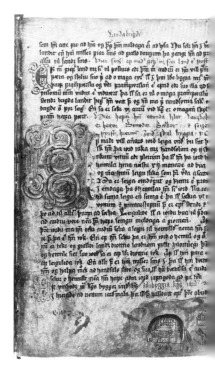

In some manuscripts there are entertaining drawings in the margin. These give some information about cultural history, though they may not of outstanding artistic merit.

Arnamagnean Collection, Copenhagen No. 345, fol: Jónsbók, 16th century and the execution is evidence of a long history of development in the craft. The Icelandic parchment, on the other hand, has been discoloured by much handling, for these books were no ornamental objects. However, to compensate for the lack of the almost machinelike accuracy of the foreign craftsmen there appears in the lettering and decoration of the Icelandic manuscripts something of the fresh originality of the literature recorded in their pages. And if some of them should seem to the critical modern observer crudely executed he can endorse the words of an Icelandic book:

e Lord crucified."

amagnean Collection, Copenhagen,
. 673 a III, 4to: Book of Drawings,
h century.

Neither gleams the gold in me
Nor gaudy letters shine.
My beauty all I hold in me,
For learning makes me fine.

The Icelandic manuscripts have their tale of woe, like those of other nations. Before the days of printing they received the usage given to printed books nowadays and were worn out by reading in the same way. Copies followed, like new editions. For this reason there is now very little preserved from the earliest times: a few fragments from the 12th century; a handful of complete manuscripts and more fragmentary ones from the 13th. But the great

It is not certain whom these figures represent. The symbol of the Lamb God suggests that the principal character is John the Baptist, whose saga in the manuscript is preceded this picture. However, he is crowned with a cross which Christ alone sho wear.

Arnamagnean Collection, Copenhag No. 233 a, fol: Saga of John the Baptist and other Sagas of Saints, 1 century.

The Icelanders submitted to Hákon Hákonarson, king of Norway, in the years 1262-64. King Magnús Hákonarson presented them with a code of laws to conform with the r powers and the newer times. This code was known as **Jónsbók**, after Icelandic lawyer involved in its compilation and responsible for bringing it to Iceland. At first it was badly received by the Icelanders, w wanted to keep their old customs; in the course of time they learned t appreciate their law-book, which wa for the most part very comprehensi and carefully prepared. They were probably the first to give King Mag his nickname of "Law-mender". For many centuries Jónsbók remained virtually unchanged; a cornerstone personal rights and a guiding light dealings between men. For this rea it was copied more often than any other Icelandic work, and many of manuscripts of Jónsbók were beaut lettered and decorated. Here is a le from Skardsbók, one of the finest these manuscripts to survive.

Arnamagnean Collection, Copenhag No. 350, fol.: Jónsbók, 14th centur

majority of Icelandic vellum books date from the 14th and 15th centuries. Then paper appears on the scene and takes the place of parchment. After that less care was taken to preserve the vellum books, which were soiled and faded with age and owing to an obsolete mode of writing more difficult to read than the new paper copies. The vellum books that have survived represent only a tiny fraction of what once existed. An analogy may be found in the iceberg. Only a tenth part is above the surface. Most of it is under water, hidden from the eye of man. Yet the visible berg towers above the waterline, assuming innumerable shapes, catching the light of the sun and casting a matchless radiance over its surroundings.

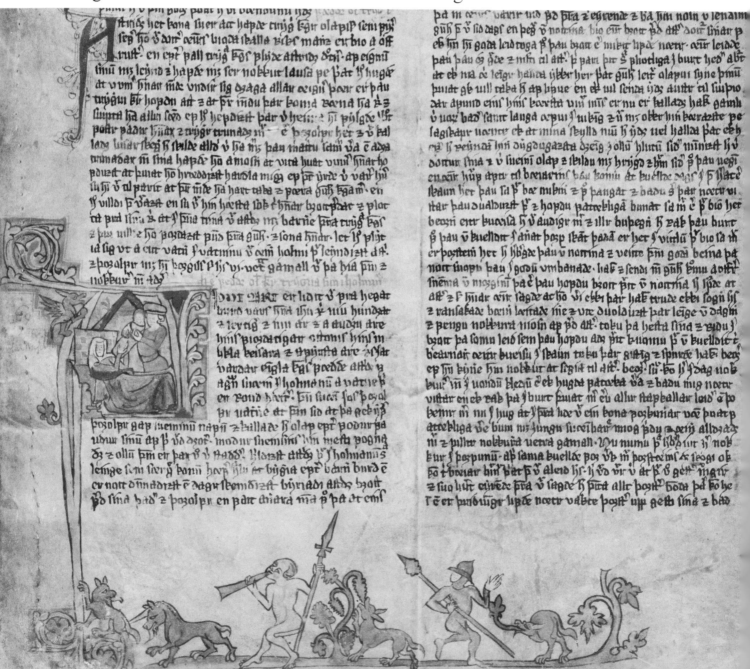

The Guardians of Norse History

Poets from Iceland presented themselves before foreign kings and recited their eulogies. In these poems they listed the battles and other noteworthy deeds of the monarchs. Thus before composing the Icelandic scald needed not only to study the art of poetry, but also to acquire knowledge about his subject. And the torch of this knowledge was passed from hand to hand: the poets stayed at court for longer or shorter periods, familiarized themselves with the king's rule, accompanied him on expeditions and composed new verses in his honour. Then they usually returned home to their own country, taking with them the new knowledge, which was preserved there in prose and verse. In this manner the Icelanders became as it were involuntary experts in the history of the northern nations. Two of the earliest existing historical works from Norway and Denmark respectively both quote Icelandic authorities. The Norwegian monk Theodoricus (Thorir) states that he is compiling his treatise on the Norwegian kings from the account of Icelanders who are of all men most learned in ancient history, deriving their lore from their ancient poems. And Saxo Grammaticus declares that he has written a substantial part of his history of the Danes from the accounts of Icelanders, who employ every moment in collecting and relaying information about the deeds of other peoples, and thus compensate for the

ok ept sint þos hiatni til þundaur vir gs hak s z se
þm til þeuonanriðu þa sir ellið um naema z bioc
augni z þa mika þe heр hur boſt ypina bu os ha
mu en van ſuo at haugbuanu ſe h haрæ ſeelþir ráð þ g
z ſuo ſleiþa þira ſuerni у ſem þyi leg ſiðan þos hianni s
agund hir egl þotbiodur ſine van þin ut þagnat la e
þa a goſþu z van alleo hallom ſagde mm mnog v vænt
gir um hnar hag hianni ggir þa til mort v ha z ſeg hi do
mi z þ hir er ho ſegiæt giæina uliæ at h ædæ þ naþin e
eu nocheunu nær um hnar hiarlſu e adſ lagde hianni þa v
bellat ſer ſiob ap at git alþur z ſleipadiæ ſbiæo v

EAR HEDIT v
þra hegat luird vr
hira ihu ept niu hund
niva ag z þirſu ær e
dlati hir hmе haup ri
riy æu en æ þyita ære
reeilhæ hira dlepn
þreddæ aſa gudband
dor ſuei barri þeþ e
er hur haрæ v ha læ
bellat ſ van v ſunne
ſuen van nepniþ ol
e h van uænic aurin i
ioi huæine h van þiæe nukill z ærguligu ſuo at hir egl oi
hiranæ z ollum hmu utвiæz ſtu mm er hiu v þaniæ unke
im uþ biagd ſueiſine huſu yþ bænlige þ v ænæiæ ug
na ſem æ lugu æt þ æugu huulikei dyno ni þi ot vd ſe v
lei veru nſæpallo loþ gude er giallda e h uveiſte oll ſina
na boſini aetum yþ ott æ egi æt haрa ollu nag m z hu
þa var halbu morua er gud bauſ h dæ ollu hielau mm o

ullkomliga framkvamduzt orð þ̄bnæðe þa goða guðs astuın[?]
or tign t̄. s̄. at hr̄ samnaðinr ot hr̄. s̄. upp timbraðe þ sama smiðe h[?]
ceılagrar tauar sem aðr v̄ gıptulıga gudvallat þ att z elskan[?]
lytur hæsta hofuðs smıðs z at lyktu gafz h sr̄ lıf z lıkama vt t̄
prelıt̄ guðs logmale z oðlaðızt þar fır margfolld þulega æs[?]
allzvalldandı guðe ollın þ tıl vendılıgr pagnaðr sem hr̄ arnaðr oð[?]
sat̄ıa z verðug en guðs nullkının at mota. Nu byrır sıga[?]
Nemr vertu sıðar baðu astu guðbrandr d. Grelot guðbrā[?]
son sends mags z anðrı sıgðr ꝥon srn̄. þ v̄ utır m̄ z auð[?]
ıgr z paðhallds ces þe. þ v̄ plærır mā vıle at dma grelot[?]
huoþangs þuıat h v̄ mceır v̄ ælþıðu skap asta byðr þ baðuı
uenzlu z morgū auðr vmū h cetr sueını ot. s kne a h v̄ þa
vı vet. z spurðe ey h leıðe nokkurn at huga hıur curuðe þra
m v̄. skılt m þ lagðe h. e betra þıkı m tıu at lırka v̄ smasueı
ua mına ıafnalldза e s huga vanda mol kalla mıa z lagðe
asta at þ se umıþm apla þn e þu hefr alldr t̄ e þo byegızt
m eıı mıebr s ey dæ gefır gua þ nokkurt at mæla þer e ek ıne
gı þ uıba vað mır epı. ot mlı huır tuıkll ecu ıuernaðr tı uı
oður h sū dæ ætıa ek tuıb þ sbeยta. ot mlı huıor māi þ betra
þıkıa at cvıga son epı þıg eðz með þu lıfðr leuðr mıa gofr
gdu eðz þn er þıoð bu er up nos. buıa mū ek þeıt gıuæı q̄
asta. ot. mlı þ seð lırð ıū poft m at dæ nuune vdæ boftur þ
teıır e aðal tır et þu muın ala eg v̄ suðu m e þu ıuert vfa
a eg v̄ þ er eglozın e з allar ueı. þ þlum mıog þm vað sıg
ur z gek h at cvıga astu. Sıgðr v̄ halfð f. sıgð l̄ hmıfa hır son
ınr harþagra. sıgðr sıū uar spekmgr mıbll gofrugr tı z a
ıdıgr en arınge uar h hmaðs. en koftıозū m v̄ h goðr veal
tır z hofs mads um alla hlutı. preddızt ot nu upp tıз sıgð
tuıp þoður sınū z astu moð smıe þ mentu olafr egs. cap. ꝯ[?]
lafr hır son v̄ sueına gıuluır m þor sınū medal m
uepstı. uıtr v̄ h sueına z oð smalır. Sıgðr en v̄ bu
sıðu tı mıbıll z harðe m smıa mıog l aıdrvın z h[?]

worldly poverty of their own with the gifts of the spirit.

Sæmund the Learned compiled a work on the kings of Norway in Latin, though this is now lost. But Snorri Sturluson says in the Prologue to his Heimskringla: "The priest Ari Thorgilsson the Learned. . .wrote, the first of men in this land, in the Norse tongue lore both old and new". And he adds "His account seems to me the most notable of all." Ari the Learned (1068-1148) was descended from a noted family of chieftains; Gudrun Osvifursdottir, the principal heroine of Laxdæla Saga, was his great-grandmother.

The Icelanders' idea of four kings of Norway: Sverrir Sigurdsson (d. 120?, his grandson Hákon Hákonarson, Magnús Hákonarson the Law-mende and Eirík Magnússon, called by som the Priest-hater.

Arnamagnean Collection, Copenhag No. 345, fol: Jónsbók, 16th century

He was brought up in Haukadal, not far from Skalholt, at the home of Hall Thorarinsson, a former friend and companion of St. Olaf of Norway, and by Teit Isleifsson, brother of Bishop Gizur, who ran a school for the clergy in Haukadal. The version of Ari's *Íslendingabók,* or Book of Icelanders, used by Snorri is now lost. But Ari rewrote it, omitting his original "lives of kings" from it, so that the work now preserved is a history of the Icelandic people only, concise but extremely reliable. Ari relies almost entirely on oral sources, but he chooses his informants with scrupulous care from among those whom he knows to be most trustworthy and have the best memories. Thus with only a single intermediary he reaches back to events that took place in the 10th century.

The second version of the Book of Icelanders narrowly escaped the fate of the first. When the age of vellum books came to an end, there was only a single half-forgotten manuscript of it surviving. This ancient manuscript came into the hands of the great scholar-bishop Brynjolf Sveinsson, who had two paper copies of it made by one of his priests, a careful transcriber of ancient manuscripts. Later the original vanished into the limbo of oblivion. After

Bishop Brynjolf's day both copies were obtained by Arni Magnusson, in whose Library they are still preserved.

Ari the Learned had also a hand in the writing of *Landnámabók,* the Book of Settlements, and probably compiled the first draft of it himself. In this work all the principal pioneers were listed, details given of the home and settlement of each, and genealogies traced from them. In existing versions the dry bones of this anthropological skeleton are given life by many short but pithy anecdotes about the settlers and their descendants. No other nation in the world can boast a comparable source-book of its origins.

The Book of Settlements had its roots in Norway with the forefathers of the first settlers, while Ari's lives of kings provided a sound basis for later works on the subject. But there is a world of difference between Ari and Snorri Sturluson. The Book of Icelanders is essentially a dry, scholarly work, its language still unpractised and a little stiff. But the latter part of the 12th century brought a remarkable advance in Icelandic historical writing. From Ari's

bald enumeration of facts there gradually emerges a wealth of narrative literature that has no equal in any other land. In other languages the Icelandic word *saga* has been adopted to describe this literature. The characteristics of saga-literature may be listed briefly: the narrative is rapid and very succint; free from verbal embellishments and verbosity. The characters are many and their characterization varied; each man has his individuality and is sketched in bold lines, and while minor characters may often be types representing particular qualities, the major ones are generally complex and enigmatic, like Gudrun Osvifursdottir and Njal of Bergthorshvol. Sometimes there is development of character, as in the case of St. Olaf in *Heimskringsla,* and Hrafnkel in his Saga. Great emphasis is laid on certain moral values and ideas, many of which are very ancient in origin, being pre-Christian and even contrary to Christian teachings. The most important concept is that of the untranslatable *drengskapr,* a word in which many virtues are implicit: truthfulness, good faith, sincerity, humanity, helpfulness, and above all courage to defend honour and family without hesitation, flinching neither at wounds nor death. The family group is a powerful defence to a man, but family ties can also be strong chains to draw him into blood-feud and vengeance, in the face of both heathen laws and Christian religion. In sagas occurring after the year 1000 men are "called Christian", as it is put, but in fact it is not the Lord of Hosts that rules their lives, but a blind, inexorable fate. Dreams and prophesies foretell future events; ghosts and other supernatural beings walk abroad. From this it may be seen that the sagas are informed with great catholicity and breadth of mind, both in their content and characterization. Each man has to answer for himself in word and deed, and each has something to be said in his favour. The dialogue is compact; often in the form of pithy aphorisms. When appropriate, speeches are put into the mouths of men; especially at *things* and other assemblies. The Sagas of Kings were among the first completely

49

original Icelandic sagas to be written. After Ari the Learned, Abbot Karl Jonsson deserves a mention. He compiled the saga of King Sverrir Sigurdsson, the great rebel who ruled Norway in the last decades of the 12th century, undaunted by the excommunications of bishop and pope. The greatness and eloquence of the king emerge clearly in the saga, but so does the point of view of his antagonists; their hatred and their suspicions regarding the nobility of his descent, which appear not entirely without foundation. Thus in his breadth of mind and catholicity of view Abbot Karl anticipates Snorri Sturluson.

About the year 1200 and during the course of the 13th century many Sagas of Kings were composed, both individual biographies and synoptic reviews of longer periods in the history of nations. As their names indicate, Færeyinga Saga and Orkneyinga Saga deal with the peoples of Færo and Orkney respectively. Knytlinga Saga, a somewhat later work named after King Knut the Great and his descendants, tells of the Danes. The Swedes have no specific saga, but their history is closely linked with that of the other Norse peoples. As might be expected, most attention is paid to the history of Norway. The majority of its kings were accorded special sagas; some of them more than one. These sagas were of varying form and quality — dry and lively, factual and loaded with fantasy and the supernatural. Comprehensive works, compiled in some degree from the older individual sagas, were only partly successful. Then a great scholar and artist appeared on the scene to absorb and reconstitute all the disparate sources into one universal Saga of the Kings of Norway, from the mists of antiquity right down to the days of King Sverrir.

Snorri Sturluson was the son of a parvenu chieftain who had raised himself to a position of importance by his personal ability and determination. Snorri was fortunate, though, in being brought up in one of the greatest cultured households in the country, at Oddi in Rangarvellir in the south, by no less a person than

"Olaf Haraldsson, king of Norway." saint treads the devil underfoot in th shape of a dragon.
Arnamagnean Collection, Copenhag No. 345, fol: Jónsbók, 16th century

The kings of Norway had special for their royal guard: the so-called Hirdskrá. These also applied to members of the royal guard in Ice and were therefore copied into th Icelandic laws.
Arnamagnean Collection, Copenha No. 126, 4to: Jónsbók with Hirds etc., about 1400.

olapur · hazaldz ꜱon · norekſ konugur ·

.i.o.i noregþs
na mæne sr

ua kg̃ en halgt byd

ſar er vpphar hud

vꝛaꝛa at oli xp̃s

ce maꝛie weiꝛe

kg̃ alla kga aꝛ

hn ge var vern

s ok alla tꝰs hand

the grandson of Sæmund the Learned himself. In his adult years he battled for wealth and power, both of which he achieved. He maintained a large estate at Reykholt in Borgarfjord, controlled a number of chieftaincies, established connexions by marriage with many of the highest in the land, twice held office as Law-Speaker and spent two long periods at the Norwegian court and with other rulers abroad. In the dispute between King Hakon and Earl Skuli, Snorri supported the latter. After Hakon had triumphed and slain his kinsman, he declared Snorri a traitor and had him assassinated at his home at Reykholt one dark autumn night of the year 1241. But such is the irony of fate that before Snorri fell he had raised the kings of Norway a memorial more splendid than any other royal dynasty has ever possessed.

Snorri's Book of Kings became known in later ages from its opening words as *Heimskringla.* It begins with the Swedish kings of legendary times; then follows the dynasty across to Norway, and real history starts with Halfdan the Black and his son, the great conqueror Harald Fairhair. Each king is given his saga, in chronological order, but the most extended is that of the royal saint Olaf Haraldsson, later the arch-patron of the Norse people. The work ends at about the point where Sverrir arrives in the country. From here there was no need to supplement the existing history of Abbot Karl.

In his Prologue Snorri gives some account of his sources and method of work. Of historical writers, only Ari the Learned is mentioned by name, but next to him the verses of the court poets are rated most highly, as contemporary authorities. "It is the practice of scalds to praise him most whom they are then before. But none would dare tell him of deeds of his which all hearers knew to be but vanity and lies, and he himself as well; for that would be mockery and no praise."

Some of the works used by Snorri have survived. It invokes one's admiration, inviting comparison with Shakespeare, to see how he contrives to breathe life

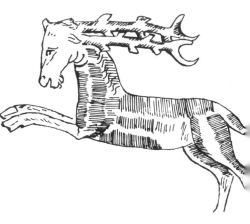

Reindeer did not exist in Iceland in ancient times, but were imported fr[om] Norway in the late 18th century. Th[e] artist would thus never have set eye[s] on such a creature.

Arnamagnean Collection, Copenhag[en] No. 345, fol: Jónsbók, 16th century into the dry bones of his material. Yet at the same time he was a more critical historian than any of his predecessors, with the exception of Ari. However, *Heimskringla* dazzled to such a degree that after its appearance on the scene the older sagas were often neglected and lost. And where Snorri adapted passages from another saga, his improvements have frequently been introduced into the original work. This applies, for instance, to parts of Jomsvikinga Saga and Orkneyinga Saga.

The number of manuscript copies also gives a good idea of the high estimation in which *Heimskringla* was held. When the systematic collection of manuscripts began in later centuries it had survived in its original form in three complete vellum books, beside fragments of a number of others. Two of these books were in the possession of the University of Copenhagen and were lost, together with all its library, in the great fire of 1728. Fortunately, though, careful paper copies had been made of these before. The third vellum book, the so-called *Frisbók,* came into the hands of Arni Magnusson and escaped destruction. The saga of St. Olaf is wanting in this text, owing to the fact that this saga existed as an independent work in other manuscripts, whose owners would therefore have it omitted from copies of *Heimskringla* itself. The separate St. Olafs Saga enjoyed the prestige of its saintly hero and existed in many manuscripts. Another indication of the popularity of *Heimskringla* may be mentioned. In the 14th century it was very much the fashion to amalgamate earlier historical works, including Sagas of Kings, and the sagas of *Heimskringla* were then invariably used as the basis of the synoptic works, with material from other sagas added. The greatest of these is the famous *Flateyjarbók,* written in the late 14th century and finally presented to the king of Denmark by Bishop Brynjolf Sveinsson. Thus either in its entirety, or by individual sagas from it, original or supplemented, *Heimskringla* is represented in the Middle Ages in more manuscripts than any other Icelandic historical work.

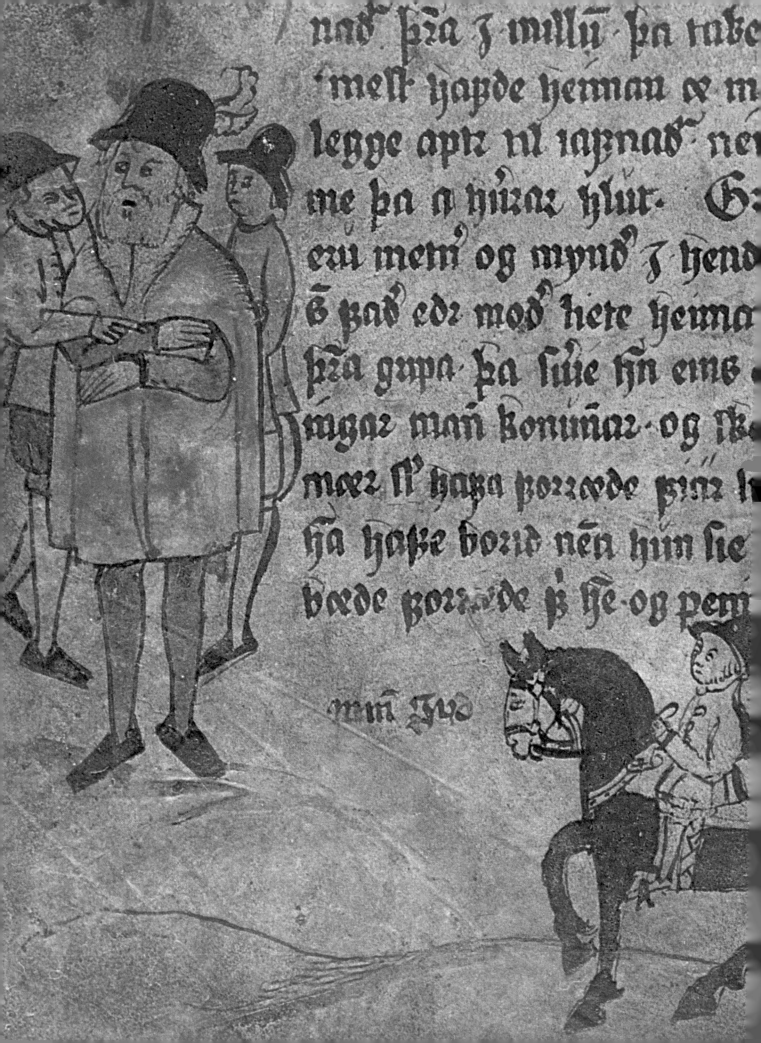

naf þra i millu þa take
mest haþde herman æ m
legge aptr til iafnaþ. nei
me þa a hivraz hlut. G:
eru meti og mynd i hend
ß þad edr mod hete herma
þra gripa þa silie hn einb
agar man bonumar og ske
mær ſ haþa boræde þraz h
ha haþe borið nen hun hie
bæde boræde þ ſie. og peri

mun gud

aʒ oſkiptu arþe iaþn mit þie ſem ſu er
uınʒt til. En eʒ þie edr arþi uınʒt e͛
uære meıra hennangiezid en ſlıkr bue
aller ͛ ħiedn e͛ til hennanþylgın og
͛ konu þær og a ħın þa iaþnħeimıla
na En eʒ ħın ſeıg͛ ad ħın ħede e͛ til þs
ʒarl ın ͛ kona og ſæþe til iaþnmilb gipt͛
til gıoʒ ħar ept͛ neıre til rnuſu. Engı
þe en ħın e͛ xx uetra gomul þo ad vnd
mþ brænda rade og a ſa er ħæ þa þær
ħær. Hu ͛ giptıng͛ ın er nettr ad konu

In what respect does Snorri excel all other authors of Sagas of Kings? The magic of great literature is always hard to explain, though perhaps a few features may be suggested. Snorri is realistic, as can be seen from his ruthless rejection of the fulsome hagiography formerly associated with the missionary kings of Norway, Olaf Tryggvason and St. Olaf. He possesses a superb dramatic gift; outlines a host of characters in clear, decisive strokes; creates living images; presents powerful opposing forces in perfect equilibrium. The vivid illusion of reality, the actuality of persons and events, cause us involuntarily to believe *Heimskringla* more readily than any other

Sagas of Kings. Snorri's art and critical spirit are united in a single creative act when he transforms himself, as it were assuming the flesh and blood of the characters severally introduced upon his stage. One example may be given here: Olaf Haraldsson has been driven from the country by the superior power of the great landowners. He musters a force in Sweden and comes back to reclaim his kingdom. Soon he is destined to fall on the bloody field of Stiklastadir, and be raised up a saint. Before the battle, though, Snorri makes a Danish bishop in the ranks of his enemies hold forth in a powerful oration in which the crimes of King Olaf's whole life are listed and his army described as a rabble of foreign robbers and bandits. After this speech the reader is left convinced that a martyr's death alone can save the good name of this luckless tyrant.

From a hypercritical modern point of view one can

Horse-fights are often described in t sagas, and were frequent occasions dispute. However, an attempt was made to prevent this by legal provisions. Here at the beginning of the section "Of horse fights" – five lines from the bottom – we read: "Wherever men goad a man's horse fight without his leave, compensatio for damage done and for malice sha be paid, according to judgment, to owner of the horse, but if there is damage of half a mark, compensati shall be paid, according to judgmen as for grave insult for what was do out of enmity and malice; but each man shall be answerable for himsel horse fights."

find fault with Snorri's history in various ways. He is not interested in social, but only personal factors. He does not hesitate to manipulate his sources in accordance with his own judgment, or even invent whole chapters to clarify and breathe life into his narrative. But by the lights of his times this was the correct historical method — and in fact there is a good deal to be said for it. In combination with poetic vision and dramatic skill, Snorri contrives to apply to his sources a keenly critical scrutiny and a rational understanding of the logic of history. *Heimskringla* has often appeared in Norwegian translations, becoming a kind of national Bible of

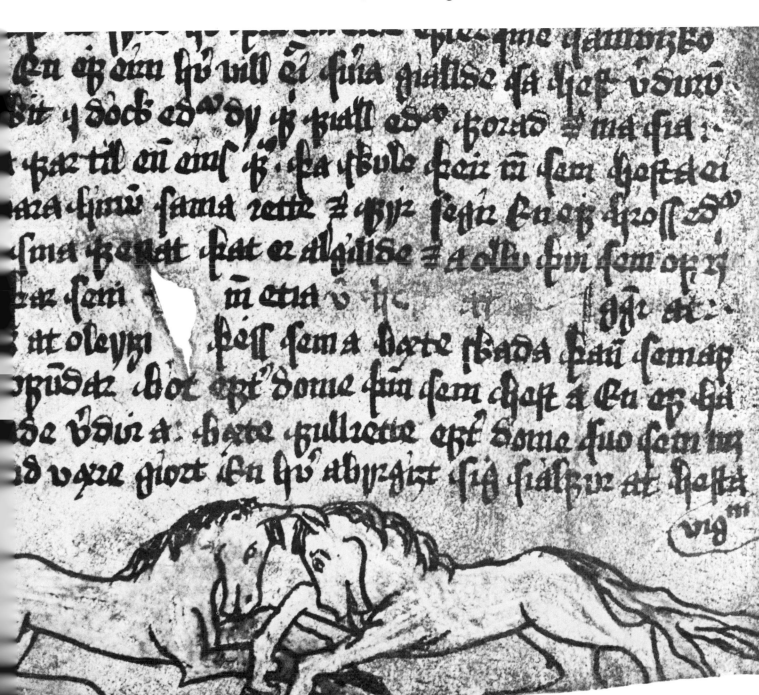

the Norwegians. It was their greatest inspiration in their struggle for national emancipation in later years, just as the Sagas of Icelanders were to the Icelandic people, raising their spirits to aspirations of freedom and independence. It was thanks to Snorri Sturluson, more than to any other single man, that, after five centuries of subordination, the Norwegians once more acquired a king of their own, who took the name of the man who in years gone by had once had the saga-farmer of Reykholt put to death.

Beaching the boat. In some manuscripts of Jónsbók initial letters are adorned with pictures illustrating the subject-matter of the subsequent section of law. Here there is an entwined motif in the initial, while pictures in the margin indicate that these are laws concerning seafaring.

Iceland's Heroic Age

Among the most remarkable and at the same time most individual of Icelandic achievements in ancient times were the Sagas of Icelanders. In the Sagas of Kings accounts of Icelanders occupy a large place, since they were both characters in the story and historical sources. Sometimes these accounts become brief, more or less independent sagas, in which case they are described as *Islendingathættir,* or Tales of Icelanders. Some of these are masterpieces in miniature; for example, the story of Audun of the Westfjords, who presented the king of Denmark with a Greenland polar bear and was generously rewarded in return, but considered himself most indebted to the king of Norway, who had given him leave to travel unhindered to a land with which he was at war. The short tales are followed by longer sagas with their setting mainly in Iceland.

There are many problems regarding the making of these sagas. All their authors are unknown. We cannot tell to what extent they were based on oral narratives — still less evaluate the traditions behind the written sagas. However, since the Sagas of Icelanders are the offspring of the Sagas of Kings, there is every likelihood that, as in the case of the latter, the oldest of the former were based on a heritage of oral sources. The style of narration is exactly the same in both groups, with variations due to the variety of authors, but shaped by the verbal art

61

of the storyteller. Many Sagas of Icelanders contain
ancient verses to confirm their narrative, much as the
eulogies are used in the Sagas of Kings. Sturla

Thordarson, Snorri's nephew, wrote a history of his own times in the 13th century which is very accurate and objective. In his more advanced years he compiled a special version of the Book of Settlements, known after him as *Sturlubók,* and supplemented it with material from later Sagas of Icelanders. This shows that in Sturla's day these sagas were considered historical.

But the Sagas of Icelanders underwent great changes in the course of time. The distance from the events of the Saga Age increased and the substance of the oral traditions grew accordingly thinner, at the same time becoming less trustworthy as raw material. To compensate, this genre of literature began to acquire an independent life of its own; one author learned from another and historical themes and tricks of style are repeated without reference to oral tradition. This development can best be demonstrated by example. The dates of composition of the sagas are not known with certainty, but roughly speaking they cover a period of about half a century. The earliest of the longer Sagas of Icelanders is probably *Heidarvíga Saga,* written near the end of the 12th century. This saga describes the conflict between the men of the Hunavatn district of the north and the men of Borgarfjord in the west that took place about the beginning of the 11th century. The decisive battle was fought on the upland heath between the two districts. Hence the saga's name. In the earlier part of it the individual killings and events leading up to the battle on the heath are traced at length.

There is every probability that the saga was based on substantial oral traditions; nevertheless it bears the marks of literary composition and a creative author. For instance, the dialogue is often in the form of long speeches which could certainly not have been transmitted by oral tradition, while some events occurring in other countries seem to have been invented by the author. The language and construction of the saga is stilted and often clumsy; there is a great deal of repetition and verbal maladroitness; the order of events is confused;

Ladies in festival attire; contempora
of the gentlemen seen on page 56
above.

Arnamagnean Collection, Copenhag
No. 345, fol: Jónsbók, 16th century

The manuscripts of the Sagas of
Icelanders contain little decoration,
probably because there was no
precedent for the influence of forei
illumination here. Kálfalækjarbók, w
is unfortunately badly damaged, is
among the few exceptions.

Arnamagnean Collection, Copenhag
No. 133, fol: Njáls Saga, manuscrip
named after the farm Kálfalækur,
written about 1300.

characters appear without introduction and out of context. Nevertheless the content of the saga is often impressive. Characterization is not as elaborate as the characters are many, but the leading persons are endowed with unity and consistency. Some of the description has a primitive grandeur reminiscent of certain primary works of other nations such as the Iliad. To give an example: Bardi Gudmundsson, leader of the northerners, has killed one of the men of Borgarfjord, and the brother of the dead man has borne his body home to their father's house. At the meeting on the heath Bardi dares both father and son to take vengeance: "How is it, Ketil? Do neither you nor your father think you have anything to avenge against us? I remember, Ketil, a short while ago you went home bringing your father a burden on your back. And if you have forgotten, here is a witness: this same sword on which the brains are still not dry" — and he shakes the sword at him — "Do you think you have nothing to avenge, Ketil, and you see here that the brains are not dry?"

Egils Saga displays evidence of a great advance in

Making the punishment fit the crim Under the law of the republic (Grág no provision is made for either corp or capital punishment. The worst offenders were condemned to outlawry; as it was termed: "unfeedable, unferriable, unfit for a help and shelter." However, accord to Jónsbók thieves were to be fine flogged for their first offences, whi inveterate offenders were to be hanged.

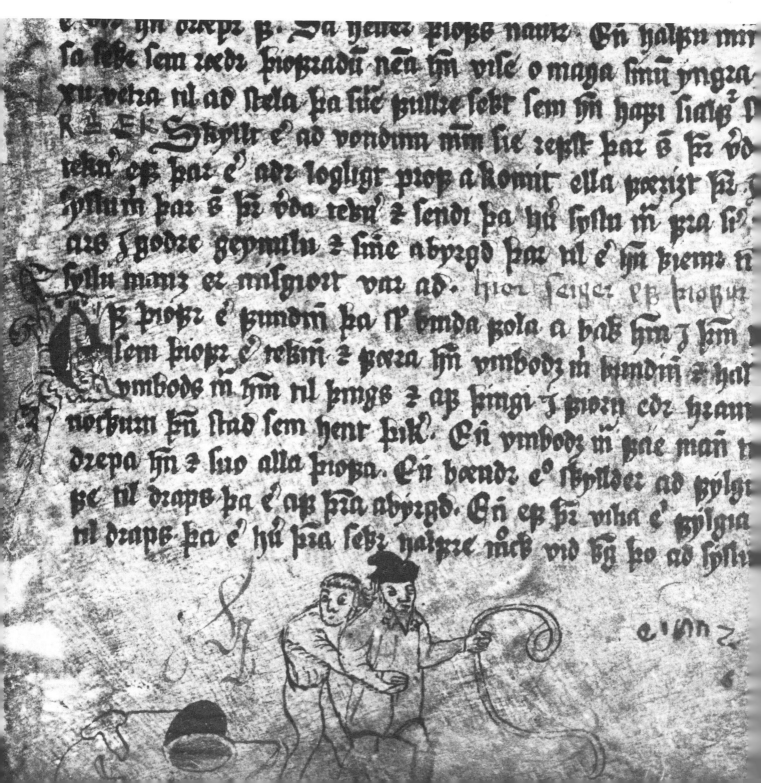

narrative technique since Heidarviga Saga. It is supported by ancient verses, for Egil was the leading poet of his age in Iceland. It can also be taken as certain that oral traditions survived, to some extent associated with the verses, concerning this great viking of the sword and the spirit. But the difference here is that now the pen is in the hand of an autonomous and skilled author who subjects his sources to the power of art. The presentation of Egils Saga is much closer to spoken narrative than that of Heidarviga Saga, but this is not because the author of the former had more oral traditions at his disposal, so much as because the gap between mouth and hand has narrowed; the saga-writer has learned from the masters of the spoken word.

In Egils Saga the author's attitude towards his material is at once scholarly and creative. Edification and art, realism and fantasy, perform a see-saw in delicate equilibrium. In this respect Egils Saga very much resembles *Heimskringla;* indeed it has long been surmised that Snorri was the author of both works. Similarities of style and vocabulary have been pointed out. There is the same catholicity of mind and self-identification of the author, the same dramatic skill, the same ability to create a tension of opposites and view events alternately from the standpoint of opposing parties. The sons of Hildirid slander Thorolf Kveld-Ulfsson, who is "popular with all men", to Harald Fairhair, and they present their case so skilfully that the reader is filled with doubts — like King Harald.

Or, to take another example: Egil becomes involved in a quarrel with Eirik Bloodaxe, son of Harald Fairhair, insults him by setting up a "pole of shame" against him, and slays his son. Eirik is later driven from Norway and takes refuge in England, where he resides with his queen Gunnhild in the city of York. With them is Egil's old friend and kinsman by marriage, Arinbjorn. And hither comes Egil, driven by a magic storm raised by Gunnhild, and is shipwrecked at the mouth of the Humber. He has no choice but to place himself at the mercy of King

Eirik. Gunnhild now urges Eirik to have him put to death on the spot, and enumerates his crimes in bitter words. But Arinbjorn defends his friend with great eloquence, finally turning his conciliatory words into a threat: "Nobody is going to call King Eirik a bigger man for killing a foreign farmer's son who has put himself at his mercy. But if he wants to win fame of this deed, then I shall do him the service of making it a tale more worth the telling; for Egil and I shall so serve one another, that both of us will have to be dealt with at the same time. Then Egil's life will cost you dear, King, when we are all laid in the dust, I and my followers."

Arinbjorn advises Egil to compose a poem in praise of King Eirik, and in one night he produces a twenty-verse eulogy in a completely novel metre. The next day he recites the poem before the king and receives the gift of his own head in reward. After this, his poem is known as Höfudlausn — "head-ransom".

Egil Skallagrimsson is the most rugged and powerful character in old Icelandic literature. In appearance he is like his father and grandfather; big, ugly and bald at an early age, and from them, too, he inherits his troll-like nature. But underneath a rugged and taciturn exterior he also conceals the splendid qualities of the two Thorolfs — his uncle who was killed by Harald Fairhair and his brother who fell in the army of King Athelstan at the battle of Brunanburgh. In his blood there burns a wanderlust that is hard to quench. Odin has endowed him with the gift of poetry to console him for the tragic loss of brother and sons. In his bed he dreams of the lovely woman once married to the magnificent Thorolf — and later wins her. He is a strange blend of divine inspiration, human sensitivity, and brutal coarseness and greed. It would be preposterous to suppose that such a personality could have emerged, as it were of its own accord, from the accounts of generations. Only a creative genius like Snorri Sturluson could have fashioned his choicest hero in so unprepossessing a form — and still made him

Disputes and blood-feuds were common in ancient times, though attempts were made to curb this cu by law. Here we see the beginning o the fourth section of the code, deali with personal rights and peace.
Arnamagnean Collection, Copenhag No. 350, fol: Jónsbók, 14th century

In later ages it was thought for a ti that the halberd (atgeir) of Gunnar Lithend was something like the we wielded here by the man against th lion, though this idea was based o misunderstanding. Such lethal instruments were unknown in Icela in the Saga Age, though they were familiar in the 16th century.
Arnamagnean Collection, Copenhag No. 147, 4to: Jónsbók, 16th centu

i norðlendinga þriðung. ok manað
um sunnlendinga þriðung. sex uik
um vestfirðinga þriðung. siðan h
kemr i syslu sina eptir rettri tiltolu.
þa at fleiri se syslum i hinum þrið
ungi en eiN. Eigi sua sokn i syslu m̄
fleiri en fiorð i þriðungi hinum. en
tueir þar sem syslu m̄ sitr i þriðungi.

¶ Þat er þ boðit at þr se
lens m̄ sem æ e fullueðia eptir at bæ
ta þ sem þr taka urettliga utan be
nd samþyckt aður. H segir um ret u
p utlendi m̄ uanlendra maNa
urða m̄ ꝛ skeina eða frendr
komir m̄ ꝛ m̄. huilu maðr ual
fir loð m̄ eigu sins rettar at krefia
af uilldum m̄. þa er nal ef þr sett
at scalf sin i milli. ella kieri sa sik þ
syslu m̄ sem uphaldiN er.

En h gau rett af hiuN urlða m̄ e lig
ligr uarð þ olaps ok þr. s se þm h
inum uildum m̄ rett gort ef þm
er rangt gort. En ef syslu m̄ þ uena
rett at gaua. þm sem uanhaldiN er
þa suari h sektiN ꝛ dæmi logiN ꝛ sky
nsam m̄ með þm sin i milli. ok slikt
sem dæmir. taki sa af þing þar kau
pum nær s. slikt sem syslu maðr aa

kialst s til er þ heꝛ sin þullt. En sys
lum heimti sin af þim eða misti ella.
En styriN sa er þa flyr bot i þorboði
sekiz þrioN morkum uið kg. huart se
neldr eiN eða fleiri. ok takiz i moti
su sekt kgi til handa. m̄ þ moti at
syslu m̄ uilldi h e rett af gaua.

¶ Þat er fullkomliga þ boðit at
styri siN eða liðs m̄ taki aðr huarir
samheldri m̄ s m̄. þe sektiN at kau
pa eðr seha dyrra uarning siN en s
sem kaupi eðr sali semia sin i milli.
En sa er at sliku uirð uirkis fastr su
ari slikri sekt kgdomunum sem haN
seN uidulogu m̄ eiN hun.

¶ Stefnu þ letia u skip þ heꝛ auit ok
eptir til kaupa uið kaupm. ꝛ seli þar
hand hendi.

¶ Vm skuldoꝛ
kaupm. sekiz half mork fyr hund
rað hitt þ sem e er golldit at olaps
þu huN fyrri halft kgi en halft þ
er skullda æ. H heꝛ
up þiN þriðia hu[n]
loghbok e heit maðr
helgr ok s husunu
þegngilldi kr m̄
at er þst maNhel
gi uarti at uar landi þiur moregs

tower head and shoulders above other men.

Laxdæla Saga is only a little later than Egils Saga, yet the style here is quite different. The characters of Laxdæla have something of the flavour of the poetic heroes and heroines of the Edda. Gudrun Osvifursdottir is Brynhild reincarnated. She cannot have the hero she desires, so she eggs on her husband to kill her beloved. The novelty in Laxdæla is the influence of the Sagas of Chivalry, then being translated into Norse from the French *chansons de geste* at the instigation of King Hakon of Norway. From these the characters of Laxdæla have their beauty, courtesy, gay clothing and romantic sentiments. Kjartan Olafsson is "the fairest of men born in Iceland", his hair is "fine as silk, falling in locks". This is something rather different from his grandfather Egil Skallagrimsson! Kjartan's wife dies of grief when she hears of his death. After Gudrun has lost four husbands and gone into retirement, her son asks her whom she had loved the most. At first she is evasive, but finally replies, with winged words: "To him was I worst, whom I loved the most."

The southern romantic stream continues to flow through the Sagas of Icelanders, side by side with the ancient Icelandic one. *Gunnlaugs Saga* begins with a symbolic dream in which Helga the Fair appears in the shape of a swan, while two eagles fight for her with sharp talons, until both fall dead. The saga follows the same pattern, owing its popularity rather to the romantic tragedy of its content than any outstanding skill of composition. However, at the same time the ancient Icelandic realism still holds the field, as in *Hrafnkels Saga,* a cautionary tale about the proud and obstinate chieftain who is brought low by his violence, learns humility from bitter experience, and rises to honour anew through his resolution. However, he has not learned his lesson well enough, but strikes again, and strikes hard, when the moment of vengeance comes.

Gradually the ancient oral sources from the Heroic Age dry up, but in their place the authors dip deeply into the wells of literature. Fantasy and romanticism

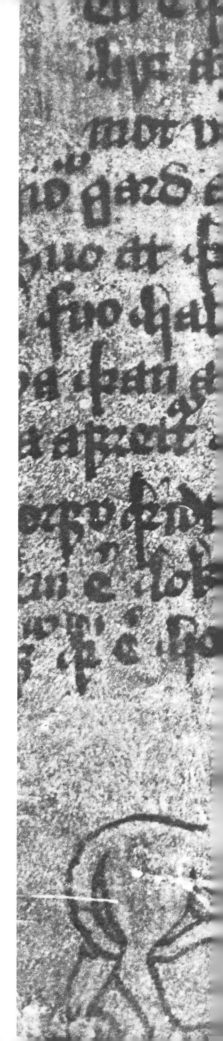

til fio̅ ... ð emmanas ...
... til gard h[l]as̅ ... e apcot ...
endæ magne suo sem þv h ...
... halfan en sa halfan sem ...
... fidan þv k n sa sem er vill ...
sui kyræ illka hia ... ir ... e suo a...
... lopad ... oll þv e kysa dagi
til kæse e m̅ vina dotir sina ...
... uæges ... til ... luuo þv e
... til þes ... hiarne

flourish. Sagas of Icelanders with little basis in tradition are invented from earlier models.

At the point of transition into the realm of pure fiction stands *Grettis Saga,* about the strong but unlucky outlaw who is blown about like a straw by the wind of a cruel fate — and *Njals Saga,* the greatest and most celebrated Saga of Icelanders of them all.

Njala has been likened to a fruit that is so sweet because it is at the point of over-ripeness. The author makes some use of oral traditions and written sources on the persons and events of the saga, but in default of any other, he helps himself liberally to

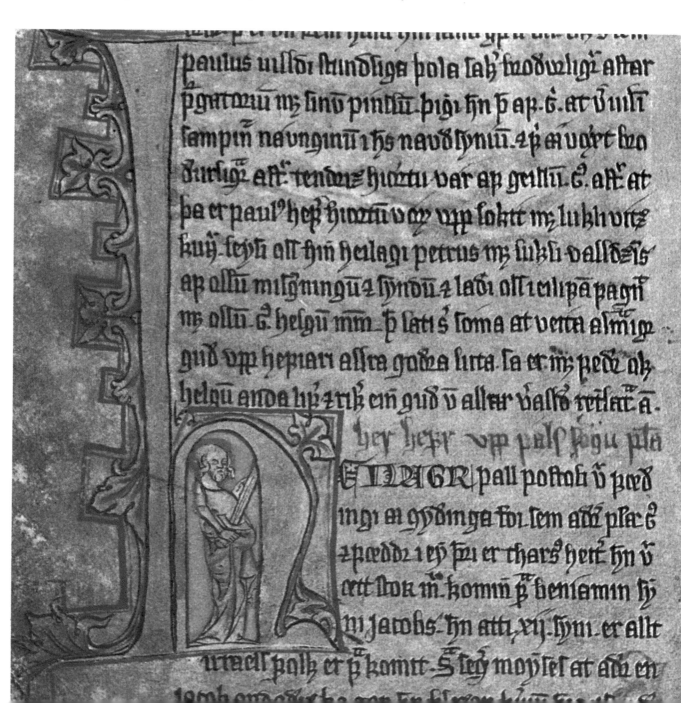

literary material, adopts whatever suits his purpose, reshapes it, and uses it in a new context in his story. The saga contains a multitude of characters and a few chapters are highly episodic. Many of the characters are exaggerated; many events melodramatic. The author shows admiration and affection for some of his persons; contempt and hatred for others. Nevertheless, the action is all logically constructed, even with long antecedents, and all the characters are sharply delineated; the dark ones with some lighter traits, and none so bright that they are without their shadows. Few works in world literature offer such a wealth of living individuals, such variety of characterization and plot, such wisdom of content.

Although *Njala* is long and complex, it is a unity from start to finish. It may be compared with a great sea of alternating waves and still water. In each individual episode of narrative there is a rhythm, a rise and fall; opposing characters are brought into collision; but after the storm comes calm and peace. The episodes are arranged in larger acts, and within the acts there is also a rhythmic movement; the waves mount higher and higher, until the mightiest billow of all comes crashing down. And after those breakers follows the greatest calm.

The first part of the saga might be named after Gunnar of Hlidarendi, though Njal of Bergthorshvol is the second leading character in it. Nothing can mar their friendship. Not even the enmity of their wives, who take it in turn for a while to have each other's house-servants and friends dispatched. Bergthora, the wife of Njal, is described as "a brave heart and somewhat hard in temper". Hallgerd, Gunnar's wife, is the character for whom the author has the strongest antipathy, and yet she is quite unforgettable.

Gunnar is a perfect "knight", a dashing figure who can jump his own height in full armour and the best of bowmen, but he also has enough crudeness and obstinacy in his make-up to be human. He is a man of peace, yet is drawn into one bloodfeud after

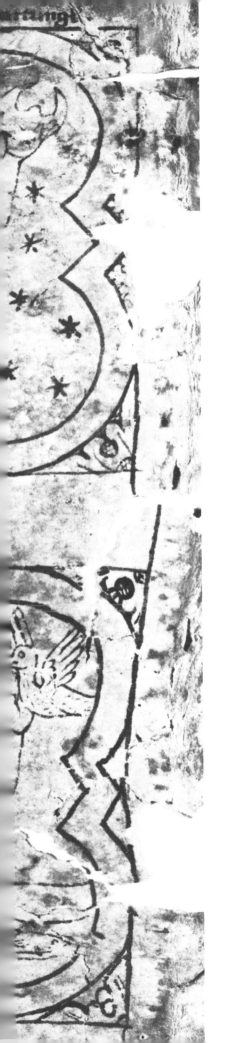

another. When he discovers that Hallgerd has been guilty of theft, he boxes her ear. He is condemned to exile for his slayings, but turns back when his horse stumbles and he happens to look up at the hillslopes above his home. "Fair is the Slope, and never has it seemed so fair to me; the cornfields pale and the meadows mown. And I shall ride home and go nowhere." But the saga offers another explanation for Gunnar's turning homeward, namely, that he will not give in to his enemies. Nor does he have long to wait before they pay him a visit. He defends himself for a long time with his bow, but when the bowstring is severed he bids Hallgerd give him a lock of her hair to twist into another. "Does much depend on it for you?" she asks. "My life depends on it," he replies, "for they will never get the better of me while I can use my bow." "Then I shall now remind you of the box on the ear you gave me, and I care not whether your defence be long or short." And after that his defence is short.

The good counsel of Njal, the wise and foreknowing, cannot save Gunnar. In the second part of the saga, though, his skill as a counsellor and his guidance are put to an even severer test. His son Skarphedin, the warrior with an ironic smile on his lips and a flaw in his heart, slays Thrain Sigfusson for little cause. To confirm the truce, Njal adopts Thrain's son Hoskuld, comes to love him as his own, and in the fullness of time confers on him a chieftainship and a splendid marriage. Njal is in the same position as Odin: he knows of the doomsday that must come, and tries to avert it, but all to no avail. Mord Valgardsson, the Iago of the tragedy, slanders Hoskuld to the sons of Njal, with the sequel that he falls at their hands like a Christian martyr. Still Njal tries to preserve the peace and avert new perils, though now it is open to question whether his whole heart is in the part he is playing. Still the clouds pile up; the storm approaches. Hoskuld's widow urges her uncle in a cruel manner to take vengeance; Flosi attacks Bergthorshvol with a large force, and Njal and his sons are burned inside. Bergthora is offered the chance of escape, but she rejects it. "Young was I given to Njal, and I promised him that one fate should fall on both of us." Between them, in their bed, they take Thord Karason, their young grandson, to die with them.

But one man escapes from the fire. This is Kari Solmundsson, the boy's father and their son-in-law. The last part of the saga deals with the consequences of the burning and Kari's revenge for his kinsfolk. Here we have the receding tide after the climax of the burning. But in this concluding section there are many lesser climaxes, becoming smaller as the end approaches, until an utter peace descends upon the scene, and the reader emerges, like Kari, purged by fire, from the catharsis of the tragedy.

The popularity of *Njala* may be judged, like that of Snorri's works, from the number of copies surviving. In all there are nearly sixty *Njala* manuscripts in existence, either complete or fragmentary. Of these, twenty-four are vellum books, or fragments of them, the earliest dating from around 1300, or not much later than the date of composition of the saga itself. No other Saga of Icelanders ever achieved such popularity. On a superficial level the mind of the child is absorbed by a simplicity and bold pictorial quality, while in later years the mature man can return to it repeatedly and always find new strokes of genius; new depths of wisdom. It was long considered a *sine qua non* for book-loving Icelanders to read the saga once every year. And old men still maintain, maybe with more than a modicum of truth, that in it answers for all the problems of human life are to be found.

"Then went Samson down, and his father and his mother, to Timnath, came to the vineyards of Timnath: behold, a young lion roared against him. And the Spirit of the Lord came mightily upon him, and he rent him he would have rent a kid". (Judges 5-6).

Arnamagnean Collection, Copenhage No. 673 a III, 4to: Book of Drawing 15th century.

Samson

A Miscellany of Lore

When old Icelandic literature is mentioned, one's thoughts turn first to the sagas, and especially two categories of them, the Sagas of Kings and Sagas of Icelanders. This is quite natural, for these works are a unique Icelandic achievement, and besides, the branch of literature with the strongest appeal to the modern reader. But there are other kinds of saga than these, and the writing of sagas was only one element in the considerable literary activity of the Icelanders in ancient times.

The art of writing was a living force in the life of the nation from the beginning, and thus the history of both past and present was written in turn. The last section of the Book of Icelanders is a history of the times of Ari the Learned, while the beginning of Sverris Saga was compiled from the king's own account, and after that from the accounts of knowledgeable informants. Although it is not a precise division, it is convenient to divide sagas into ancient and contemporary. The proximity of the present overcrowds the stage; faced with too great a mass of material, the writer has trouble selecting and rejecting; the fetters of fact impede the creative spirit of the artist. On the other hand, contemporary sagas are freer from fantasy, more detailed, more exact. Contemporary sagas fall into two main categories: the Sagas of Bishops and a group of sagas dealing with the conflicts and battles of secular chieftains.

George slaying the dragon and
rating Princess Cleodolinda, who
nds behind the knight and watches
combat with anticipation.

amagnean Collection, Copenhagen,
673 a III, 4to:
k of Drawings, 15th century.

These secular contemporary sagas were collected in a synoptic work, just as the Sagas of Kings were brought together in *Flateyjarbók.* This great collection of sagas and the period have both been associated with the name of the clan of which Snorri Sturluson was a member and are known respectively as Sturlunga Saga and the Age of the Sturlungs. In the 17th century there were two more or less complete manuscripts of Sturlunga Saga; one reasonably well preserved, but the other worn to shreds by gross neglect by the time Arni Magnusson recovered its poor remains. However, a number of paper copies had been made of both vellum books, so this remarkable source-document on the history of Iceland in the 12th and 13th centuries was saved. The nucleus of Sturlunga Saga is formed by the contemporary history of Sturla Thordarson, Snorri's

of the city of Jerusalem. The artist
mpts to draw and locate the
ous buildings, but has nothing to
y, apart from his own imagination
the written accounts of the Middle
s.

amagnean Collection, Copenhagen,
736 I, 4to, about 1300.

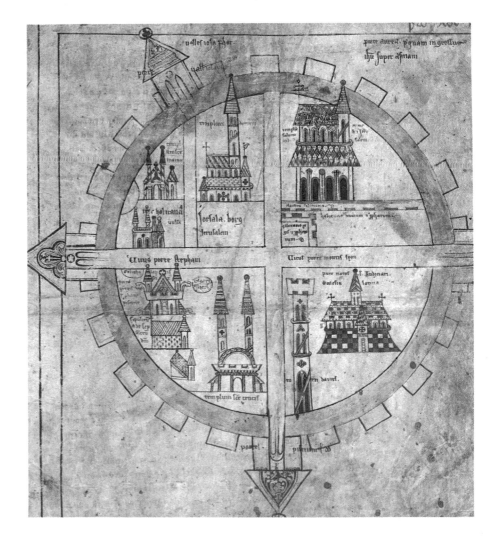

nephew. This covers the period from the end of the 12th to past the middle of the 13th century. The ancient republic had by this time lasted longer than is usual for so happy a polity, and the inexorable advance of history had uncovered its weaknesses. Under the ancient constitution the Icelanders had no common executive authority. The powers in the land, previously distributed among 39 equal godar, had now become concentrated in the hands of a few men. When these great chieftains were of a quiet and peaceable disposition, like Snorri's foster-father, Jon Loftsson, all was well. But struggles for power between them grew more frequent, and the country

was rocked spasmodically by civil conflict. King Hakon of Norway was very ready to concern himself with the quarrels of the Icelanders in order to win control over the country. In the end, exhausted by constant wars throughout the land, the Icelandic people chose as the lesser of two evils to become the king's vassals. They swore an oath of loyalty and submission to Hakon in the years 1262 - 1264. It is one of the paradoxes of history that periods of major disruption, when old societies are falling apart, are also periods of great intellectual achievement. In the death-throes of the Republic the Romans produced their greatest poets and writers: Cicero, Horace, Ovid and Virgil. In the same way the

þat mal. ꝛ gangi einir ꝼam. ꝛ þa er
ꝼir viða ꝼamðu. gangi aptr t aðnaka
ſingina. ꝛ beiði þa ꝼamþyckia ſina ti
am. En ſir ꝼe e viðia ꝼamþyckia ſiin
þ at en vitu ſir ꝼamaka en ſir ꝼegia
ella ꝼekr hiin ſna hafþ ojk við kv.
her ſeg hvſſu maðr ſkal ſig til
arþs þiara. en þeſi capitule a at
ſtanða eᵽt erþder þir iðokeũe

Aᵘ ſeikr atviein tingum
huᵗ iĩ er arþgeingr eðr e
ſteᵽin ſin t ſigs ſa er hiin ivendi
þir arþi. þa ſir hiin mota votta ſin
na at hiin ſteᵽnði hiin ſinuey. Au
ſið þat at voᵗ bⁱa. v̈ voᵗz þ e mo
ðer þes v̈ þeit loghſiga i ſiin ſtað. ꝛ
a neᵽ ſtað. þa eigu ſmg ĩ hiin arþ
at ꝺæma. hinnitna ſiar ſe maðr ti
til ſiik t arþs þiara ſeiði votta ſina
til ꝛ ſteᵽ ſiin oðᵗ ꝛ er ſiin arþi er
naeſtr: En eᵽ þ ſteᵽnir eigi ſiin t ſia
er hs voᵗ þir ikovi̊.

Age of the Sturlungs has to its credit the fact that it was also the golden age of Icelandic literature. The upheavals and agonies of civil war released untapped energies and in the chill wind of treachery and deceit men found warmth in the ancient ideas of heroism and nobility.

Again, there are other types of saga which would be regarded as literature in their own right, were there not other and more notable kinds on offer. Sagas of chivalry were originally translated in Norway from the French *chansons de geste,* as mentioned earlier. Later, Icelanders took to composing their own Sagas of Knights, partly under the influence of the Norwegian translations, but utilizing very varied material. Another class of saga has its setting in Scandinavia in the times before the settlement of Iceland. These Legendary Sagas existed in oral form and were told for entertainment, though for a long time they were not considered fit material to be recorded on parchment. But once the fantasy of the Sagas of Knights had prepared the way, these homemade diversions also came to be written down. In printed editions the Legendary Sagas are grouped together under the Icelandic title *Fornaldarsögur Nordurlanda* (sagas of ancient times in the Nordic lands). The Icelandic Sagas of Knights and Legendary Sagas were mostly written in the 14th and 15th centuries. The ancient Icelandic commonwealth had come to an end and the nation was heading into the dark ages of poverty and oppression. Literature then becomes a dream world, beyond the misery and suffering of everyday life.

Finally, there is one other group of sagas of substantial volume which should be mentioned. They are the sagas about the Virgin Mary and other saints

Two marvellous beasts from Physiologus. "There is in the sea a whale called Aspedo... When he is hungry he opens his mouth and em[...] as it were a sort of perfume. And t[...] little fishes smell the perfume and gather into his mouth. But when hi[s] mouth is full, he closes it and swal[...] them."

Arnamagnean Collection, Copenhag[en] No. 673 a II, 4to: Physiologus, abo[ut] 1200.

of the Church, known collectively as Sagas of Saints. These came to Iceland with the Christian faith, first in Latin, but translated into Icelandic at a very early date. Sometimes material from several sources would be combined, or the story retold to suit the literary taste of a later age. Thus varying versions came into being. The men of the Reformation considered it pleasing to God to destroy as many books crowded with Popish error as they could. Nevertheless a surprisingly large number of manuscript Sagas of Saints managed to survive. The love of books of the Icelanders was stronger than religious fanaticism. But the sagas could never have become what they did

bird there is in the River Nile that is ed Hidris. (Physiologus) records of it t it kills the kokodrillus. It is the ure and custom of it, when it sees kokodrillus sleeping, it daubs itself n mud and runs into the mouth of kokodrillus as it sleeps on the bank he river, and rends and tears it all in, piercing its belly, until it is d."

in Iceland without a flowering of culture in other fields. Icelanders pursued other branches of learning and the arts then prevailing in civilized countries and had notable achievements to their credit in fields apart from saga-writing. In the printed catalogues of the libraries in Copenhagen the ancient manuscripts are classified under 18 main headings, according to content, with several sub-headings in each. The sagas comprise only one of four groups listed in the catalogues under the name *"Historie"*. Admittedly it is the largest group. The second largest consists of various kinds of verse among which the Eddic poems tower above the rest in terms both of poetic value and of cultural history. Next in volume are the legal works, with the ancient codes of law themselves, both from the old republic and especially later ones from the period of the monarchy, forming a nucleus. There is also a variety of theological works in large quantity, as well as stories and poems about the saints.

Worthy of special note is the fact that the Icelanders excelled in various branches of science. The priest Bjarni the Mathematician, who lived in the 12th century, wrote a treatise on chronology. His elder contemporary was one known as Star-Oddi who made observations on the movement of the sun which are considered unique for this period. Nor has the unknown author of the First Grammatical

Abraham sets out for the land of Canaan with Lot, his nephew.

Arnamagnean Collection, Copenhag No. 226, fol: Stjórn, 14th century.

John the Baptist with the Lamb of God.

Arnamagnean Collection, Copenhag No. 233 a, fol: The Saga of John th Baptist and other Sagas of Saints, century.

al huggana
andlan ok þ
ok uegsemd
sem ser sonr
ar horðu gt
rettu gilali
Sidan gvuðu
neskur hiur
a siðan ok s
as skurd go
gt sak þiod
n helur her
maria hur
urd goð bel
ar huslin A
eguðu in
a up er þa

hare ga
m nadho
tuna sen
seautugi
uar ella
hachm þ
ram uar
gat at e
bon lo
ray ok u
vadiz i þ

gnu voftr landi. challdea sem nu h

Treatise any equal in his field for originality and independent observation.

The sagas should not be treated as a mysterious and isolated phenomenon, but should be considered in conjunction with other branches of culture, both in Iceland and the surrounding world. The basis of saga-writing was a sound national economy, varied intellectual activity, and unbroken links with the cultural centres of other lands.

A Thousand Years of Living Literature

After Iceland passed under the crown of Norway the internal conflicts that had raged intermittently for half a century died down. The population could breathe more freely — for the time being. But as years went by the unhealthy effects of foreign domination became apparent. And there were other difficulties for which the administration could not be blamed. The Church gradually lost its close links with the secular powers and became just a small limb of the universal Catholic body under the Papacy, and with this the connexion between foreign culture and Icelandic lore was also loosened. Property was accumulated by the Church and a few rich men, while the masses became impoverished. Late in the 14th century Norway passed under the Danish crown, and with it Iceland, which then became a kind of outlying Norwegian croft in the eyes of the Danish authorities. Luther's reformation reached Iceland about the middle of the 16th century, in effect as a cynical profit-making move on the part of the monarchy. Most of the wealth of the Catholic Church now reverted to the king, in addition to his other income from the country. The royal agents had often been foreigners, and they exercised their authority variously. At the close of the age of the commonwealth the Icelanders had possessed hardly any ocean-going ships. After 1600 all trade was in the hands of Danish merchants. To foreign misrule were added pestilence and famine. The Black Death reached Iceland about the year 1400 and is estimated to have killed a third of the population. The polar ice repeatedly blocked the coasts, causing disastrous seasons and the death of livestock. Volcanoes emitted ash that poisoned the grazing and killed flocks all over the country, bringing starvation to the people. The worst eruption was in the late 18th century and devastated the land like the Black Death.

Remarkable as the achievements of the Icelanders had been in the age of the commonwealth, the considerable and often original literary activity of the people in the centuries of misery was scarcely less so. In the final period of Catholicism religious poems were composed, and a beginning was made to the creation of a great corpus of historical ballads from the material of the ancient sagas — the so-called *rímur,* which form a class of poetry on their own. At the Reformation translations were made into robust Icelandic of the New Testament, and later the complete Bible. Individual known poets and authors stand out, but behind them there is a mass of competent verse-makers who composed occasional poems, hymns and ballads, while scholars compiled annals and memoirs of their own times.

Evidence of the literary interest may be seen in the impressive output of manuscripts. By far the majority of Icelandic vellum books date from the 14th and 15th centuries; that is, after the country had lost its independence and the decline had set in. The manuscripts of the golden age of the republic wore out and were lost, but the large number of vellum copies from succeeding centuries shows that people could still appreciate the sagas, although the composition of new ones had more or less ceased.

At the time of the Reformation two technical novelties affecting the literature came to Iceland: the art of printing and paper. Printing was long the monopoly of the Church and the literature of Lutheran orthodoxy was for the most part light-weight. But paper, which was infinitely less expensive than parchment, came to the rescue of secular

A bishop, with mitre and crozier, introduces the laws of the Church.

Arnamagnean Collection, Copenhagen No. 160, 4to: Jónsbók, with ecclesiastical laws, etc., 15th century

literature. Skill with the pen was as common as before. The old sagas were re-copied on paper, time after time, and the whole country was like one universal scriptorium.

The beginnings of a systematic collection of manuscripts and a more exact evaluation of old texts may be traced to the Renaissance of Greek and Latin culture at the close of the Middle Ages. This movement reached Scandinavia in the form of a humanism that awakened a desire to recover the ancient history of the northern peoples. It then became evident that the sources were mainly to be found in the ancient writings of the Icelanders, still unpublished and preserved in old vellum books. The

Representatives of various nations existing in the imagination of the Middle Ages. The Cyclopes have a single seeing eye in the middle of foreheads and use it in turn. The Panotii have such big ears that the cover the whole of their bodies. Th Hippopodes live in Scythia and ha hooves like horses.

Arnamagnean Collection, Copenha No. 673 a I, 4to: Physiologus, abo 1200.

Danes and Swedes now began to compete in the collection of these manuscripts, and later in having them translated or re-written, either in their national languages, or in Latin, the language of learning. With this, the bulk of the old vellum books and many paper copies left Iceland. Some ended up in the royal libraries of Denmark and Sweden, but most were acquired by the great Icelandic bibliophile Arni Magnusson. He was a professor at the University of Copenhagen, but spent years travelling round Iceland as a powerful emissary of the Danish government. Thus he was in a strong position, both at home and abroad, to accumulate Icelandic manuscripts. He was a pioneer in the proper evaluation of sources, and there was no scrap of parchment so insignificant that he did not try to unearth and add it to his collection. Tragically, part of his collection was destroyed in the great fire of Copenhagen in 1728. However, he managed to save most of the vellum books, though his printed books and a mass of copies of documents were burned. On his deathbed Arni bequeathed his manuscripts to the University of Copenhagen, which was at that time also the university of Iceland. Copenhagen has since been the chief centre for the study and publication of ancient Icelandic manuscripts by collaboration between Danish and Icelandic scholars. Recent years have seen a most gratifying infusion of new life into these activities, with an increase of staff and finance. Even more important, the Danish National Assembly has agreed to the return of the majority of the manuscripts to Iceland, to be entrusted to the care of the young university in Reykjavik, where a special Manuscript Institute has been established to undertake the work of keeping and utilizing them. A fine building has been erected and a staff of expert scholars engaged. But the work in Copenhagen will continue. Some manuscripts will remain there, while others will be available through photographs.

When the Icelanders took up their struggle for freedom in the 19th century, they based their claims on ancient historical authorities, documents and treaties with their kings in Norway and Denmark. The ancient literature was both an inspiration to the independence movement and the mainspring of a new literary revival. The grand concepts of a long-vanished heroic age lighted the way. If the old sagas and poems had not still been a living force in the national culture, the Icelandic people could never have regained independence in the present century. The Icelandic sagas and Eddic poems are a notable chapter in the history of world culture, and the manuscripts that preserve this literature the most treasured heritage of the Icelandic people. They have therefore no more solemn duty than to guard this heritage faithfully and bring forth its fruits in new works.

Layout: Auglýsingastofan h.f., Gísli B. Björnsson.
Designer: Gudjón Eggertsson.

English translation: Alan Boucher.

Illustrations from: Arnamagnean Institute, Copenhagen, Royal Library,
Copenhagen, Royal Library, Stockholm, University Library, Uppsala, National
Library of Iceland, Reykjavík, Manuscript Institute of Iceland, Reykjavík.

Printed in the Netherlands in 1970 by Henkes-Holland N.V.